Advance Praise for
Conversations on Leadership
Wisdom from Global Management Gurus

A provocative, engaging and lively series of conversations with top thinkers that provide both inspiration and illumination for managers.

Hayagreeva Rao
Atholl McBean Professor of Organizational Behavior
Stanford Graduate School of Business

Lan Liu's book *Conversations on Leadership* is full of insights and practical advice on the nature of leadership. The book is unique not so much in its summary of leadership theories by scholars of world renown, but in its conversational approach to discussing leadership in its historical and cultural contexts with many of those who have been instrumental in shaping ideas and practice in this field. As such, this book is a valuable addition to the bookshelves of both students of leadership and corporate practitioners alike.

Dr. John Yang
Dean and Professor, Beijing International MBA Program
Peking University

Through his vivid conversations with leadership masters from both the West and the East, and through his efforts to integrate their thoughts in a way that takes them beyond the American model, Lan Liu has opened a new page in our understanding of what leadership is, what it means and the qualities required of leaders. This book will, I am sure, prove to be a great guide to anyone who aspires to lead in this global era, whatever the context.

Michael Yu
Founder, Chairman and CEO
New Oriental Education & Technology Group

Conversations on Leadership

Wisdom from Global Management Gurus

Conversations on Leadership

Wisdom from Global Management Gurus

LAN LIU

JOSSEY-BASS
A Wiley Imprint
www.josseybass.com

This edition is published by John Wiley & Sons (Asia) Pte. Ltd., 2 Clementi Loop, #02-01, Singapore 129809 on behalf of Jossey-Bass, A Wiley Imprint.

989 Market Street, San Francisco, CA 94103-1741–www.josseybass.com

Jossey-Bass books and products are available through most bookstores. To contact Jossey-Bass directly call our Customer Care Department within the U.S. at 800-956-7739, outside the U.S. at 317-572-3986, or fax 317-572-4002.

Jossey-Bass also publishes its books in a variety of electronic formats. Some content that appears in print may not be available in electronic books.

Library of Congress Cataloging-in-Publication Data
ISBN 978-0-470-82569-3

Typeset in 11/14 pt Minion-Regular by Thomson Digital, Noida, India.
Printed in Singapore
10 9 8 7 6 5 4 3 2 1

To Andi and Baqiao,
with faith that you will be the leader of your own life
and make a difference for the world

Contents

Foreword

The way I learn most effectively, I discovered long ago, is in conversation with others. It is in the playful, exhilarating, joyous thrashing out of ideas with brilliant people that my own ideas are brought to life, refreshed, and vetted. George Braque once observed, "The only thing that matters in art is the part that can't be explained." Perhaps the only thing that matters in leadership is the part that we struggle to capture and bottle. Conversation has been one of my main pathways to pursue it.

Lan Liu surprised me with this shared passion when he visited me in Santa Monica on a pleasant morning two years ago. He had made an appointment with me as a "leadership student" and also editor-in-chief of China's leading management magazine. He told me that he was going to talk to Jim Collins, Jim Kouzes and James March on the same trip; he had already spoken to, among others, John Kotter, Ronald Heifetz, Peter Senge, and Bill George when he traveled to the United States last time; and he was planning to visit Howard Gardner, Noel Tichy and more later on.

I was impressed of course, more by his charm than his ambitious and exciting plan. He was fabulous at learning from conversation. I asked him in an email later, "Do all, well, not all but do most Chinese have your whimsy and humor?" I dropped a note to my co-author Noel Tichy the very day and encouraged him to talk to Liu, "Spent an hour with him this morning and found it worthwhile. I guarantee that you will find him engaging and thoughtful."

Now with this book, which I am glad that I made a little contribution to, I find my time spent with Liu even more worthwhile as it wouldn't be just the two of us learning from our conversation. Liu has made a unique contribution by scouting around for all those extraordinary leadership thinkers, engaging them in thoughtful conversations, getting the best ideas out of them, and presenting them in a delightfully readable format. None of the above is an easy task, but all are fulfilling ones. I have to confess a principled envy of Liu's capacity to engage others. All leadership students, researchers, educators, or practicing managers and public servants who aspire to become a leader, should have this tome as a compulsory reading. "Dialog is the oldest and the most effective way of learning from a master," writes Liu. He does it well.

The second major contribution of this book is the eight disciplines of leadership Liu has summarized those thinkers' ideas into: (1) Connecting with people, (2) Learning from failure, (3) Reflecting on experience, (4) Thinking deeply, (5) Storytelling, (6) Being a teacher, (7) Knowing yourself, (8) Becoming yourself. Those *disciplines*—a word Liu has carefully, and rightly chosen to make the point that leadership requires daily practice and continuing hard work—aren't novel or fancy; I have covered many of them in my book *On Becoming a Leader*. But as evidenced in being the constant themes those thinkers hit again and again, they are the compass directing the journey of becoming a leader.

All eight disciplines are pivotal, and can't be addressed lightly. For example, although I already wrote a lot about "knowing yourself" and "becoming yourself," recently I revisited this topic in "Leadership as a Performing Art," an essay included in *The Essential Bennis*. In it I told a story about Sydney Pollack, the late Oscar-winning director who once told me that he was at a loss when he first moved behind the camera, so he simply acted like a director. "I even tried to dress like a director—clothes that were kind of outdoorsy," he said. That raises crucial questions about leadership. Can a leader be authentic, or do the masks of command force the leader to be something other than his or her true self? In becoming yourself can you both act and be real? These are questions with no easy answers. The role of a leader is usually greater than the individual and thus worth taking on. Pollack made the leader's requisite leap into the unknown and he excelled.

Liu's third big contribution is he has opened a door to the exchange of leadership thoughts between the West and the East. Few such books, if any, have brought in thinkers from China and India and made their voice as sonorous as those from the United States and Europe. As Liu points out, leadership has been to a large extent an American product, and American scholars tend to pursue a universal leadership model.

I don't think such a pursuit is completely futile. Just as there are universal laws in many other human activities, there are universal laws in leadership too. However, particularly at this era when "the world is flat," as Thomas Friedman vividly depicts for us, the cultural aspects of leadership deserve more attention from our fellow Americans, particularly those in leadership positions.

Culture isn't the only lens through which we should see leadership, but it's the one we shouldn't miss. I personally find the cultural lens provided in this book illuminating. For example, I have written about the failure of the George W. Bush presidency in the new Introduction to the twentieth anniversary edition of *On Becoming a Leader*, "One of Bush's major failings, I believe, was his overriding commitment to an ideology rather than to principled pragmatism. In foreign affairs, for example, Bush acted in the fervently held belief that democracy is universally desired and desirable and will ultimately triumph. That ideology proved particularly ill-adapted to the realities of the Middle East." Cho-yun Hsu, a Chinese historian, reminds me from this book that what I see as an ideology problem can be seen from a cultural lens and interpreted as an illustration of the Christian Golden Rule: *Do unto others as you would have them do unto you*, as opposed to the Confucian Golden Rule: *Don't impose on others what you don't want others to impose on you*. Hsu's comment is refreshing, "That is precisely the American problem. The Americans have been leading the world for such a long time, but nobody has thanked them for it. Their attitude is 'My way is the better way. You follow me.' The Chinese believe in not doing unto others what you don't want others to do unto you. This prevents you from imposing yourself; it's for toleration."

I also wrote about the economic downturn initiated by the 2008 financial meltdown, "They resulted from lack of leadership at every level, including failures by government officials and those heading the banking and financial services industries." I partly blame this to ideology as well, "because of the administration's ideological disdain for government itself, one of the of the most destructive forces at work during the Bush years was the corrosive drip, drip, drip of privatization unchecked by effective oversight. It caused the outsourcing of much of the war in Iraq, inadequate oversight of the financial sector and other industries, and the stealthy semi-privatization of Medicare and other government programs." It is enlightening to see this from a cultural lens too. Liu reminds us in the Afterword that this might be attributed to a cultural bias toward utilitarian achievement in the United States, and so it is not only a failure of leadership, but perhaps the failure of leadership of the American model.

I was inspired by my talk with Liu. I am even more inspired by the conversations he has had with other leadership thinkers. Trust me, you will be too.

Warren Bennis
University Professor and Founding Chairman
of the Leadership Institute at the
University of Southern California
His memoir, *Still Surprised: A Memoir of a
Life in Leadership* will be published in 2010

Acknowledgments

I t wouldn't have been possible for me to compile this book without the help of many people. First and foremost, I am grateful to those 13 Masters included in this book: Joseph Badaracco Jr., Warren Bennis, Debashis Chatterjee, Howard Gardner, Bill George, Cho-yun Hsu, John Kotter, Jim Kouzes, James March, Jerry Porras, Peter Senge, Noel Tichy, and Manfred Kets de Vries. They kindly shared their time and insights with me to make this book happen. I am truly honored to have had the opportunity to collaborate with this "Dream Team" in the field of leadership.

Some deserve particular credit: Warren Bennis, for introducing me to other leadership thinkers and writing a very generous foreword; Jim Kouzes, for encouraging me to pursue the idea of an English book; James March and Peter Senge, for writing a foreword for my Chinese book *Master Classes of Leadership*, which has spawned this book.

I am also privileged to have spoken to the following people on management and leadership when preparing for this book: Jim Collins, Thomas Davenport, Ronald Heifetz, Philip Kotler, Daniel Quinn Mills, Scott Snook, and Robert Sternberg. Although those conversations didn't make their way into this book, they helped me toward a better understanding of the subject of leadership.

A special note of thanks must go to Jet Magsaysay, a dear friend and mentor. He participated in this project from the very beginning by recommending candidates I should interview and made great efforts to review and edit almost each chapter before I submitted the manuscript. Aside from being a management expert, he was a great critic and editor. Professor Steven DeKrey reviewed an early version of the manuscript. His comments are deeply appreciated.

Joel Balbin, C. J. Hwu, Nick Melchior, and John Owen, of John Wiley & Sons, have worked with me closely on this book. C. J. Hwu saw the value in a cursory book proposal and helped to perfect it. Nick Melchior provided precious comments on the manuscript, and managed most of the publishing efforts as the senior editor. Joel Balbin, the production editor, made his best efforts to coordinate the production and keep the schedule. John Owen, the wonderful copyeditor, took great pains to polish the manuscript. It was really a pleasure to work with all of them.

After I shaped the idea of the Eight Disciplines of Leadership, I was able to test it as an educator at executive development programs hosted by corporations and universities. I am thankful to those program participants for providing useful feedback, and to the organizers, particularly Professor Ye Zicheng of Peking University, for offering me the opportunities.

Last, but by no means least, I would like to thank my wife, Chen Zhongzhu, for her incredible patience and solid support, and my two sons, Baqiao and Andi, for interrupting my work in various, delightful ways while I was writing this book.

The Eight Disciplines of Leadership

F ew subjects have attracted more attention yet generated more confusion than leadership. As James McGregor Burns put it in his 1978 classic *Leadership*: "Leadership is one of the most observed and least understood phenomena on earth."[1]

Misunderstandings of leadership abound. Just take one example: leadership is often regarded as heroic; therefore turnaround leaders such as Lee Iacocca at Chrysler, Lou Gerstner at IBM, and Carlos Ghosn at Nissan are highly admired. It is no wonder that many people view a post-crisis era, such as the period of the 2008–09 financial meltdown, as the greatest leadership challenge.

Yet heroic leadership could be a myth. Let me invite Bian Que, a legendary Chinese physician who lived in the Warring States Period, more than 2,300 years ago, to unveil this idea for us.

The King of Wei asked Bian Que, "You have two brothers who are doctors too. Which one of you three is the best?" Bian Que answered, "My big brother is the best. The other brother is also better than me. I am the worst but the most famous." The king was puzzled and inquired why.

Bian Que explained, "My big brother is the best doctor because he sees a disease and cures it even before the patient feels any symptoms. Yet this makes it hard for his greatness to be recognized this way. So he is only admired within my family.

"The other brother, the second best, cures a disease when it develops early symptoms that at most cause little pain. Therefore he is regarded as only good at treating minor ailments and thus enjoys a small reputation in my hometown.

"In my case, patients always come to me when their disease is at an advanced stage. They and their desperate families are so pleased when I perform dramatic measures, such as puncturing, bloodletting, poisoning, and surgery, to cure or relieve the disease. That is why I am famous across borders."

Just as the people of the Warring States Period idolized the heroic doctor, we tend to favor heroic leaders; but, as Bian Que explained, they are not necessarily the best ones. Or are they?

Leadership would no doubt benefit from more discussions similar to the dialog between the inquisitive king and the master doctor. For this reason, I asked 13 contemporary masters of leadership to talk to me in an attempt to present the best understandings of leadership in a vivid format. This group is a veritable leadership "Dream Team," which boasts the following unparalleled characteristics:

- **Authoritative** They are ranking authorities, featuring regularly in the lists of "management gurus." To name a few: Warren Bennis, who has been called by *Forbes* the "Dean of Leadership Gurus;" John Kotter, who is the foremost authority in change leadership; James March, who ranked behind only Peter Drucker as the "Gurus' Guru;" and Howard Gardner, who is one of the most influential psychologists in the world and ranked by the *Wall Street Journal* as the fifth-most influential business thinker.
- **Diverse** They represent 13—or more—unique perspectives of leadership. For example, Peter Senge advocates "learning organizations" and Noel Tichy "teaching organizations;" Cho-yun Hsu approaches leadership with history and Chinese traditions, and Debashis Chatterjee with Indian wisdom; Manfred Kets de Vries takes a clinical approach and Howard Gardner a

cognitive one. Only by combining these diverse perspectives could we get close to a panoramic view of leadership.

- **Profound** They are all thinkers. It is no accident that all are university professors who have written books to convey their thoughts on leadership in a systematic way. Bill George might appear an exception since he spent most of his career as a CEO. However, he is selected not for his performance as a CEO— although he was one of the best—but for his views on leadership, which he has developed and elaborated in a number of books. He has, by the way, been a professor at Harvard Business School for several years now.

- **Practical** Leadership, like management, is more about doing than knowing. All of our Masters offer practical advice rather than esoteric meditations from a secluded Ivory Tower. Some—like Warren Bennis as president of the University of Cincinnati, Bill George as CEO of a Fortune 500 company, and Jim Kouzes as head of a consultancy—were significant "players" themselves. All have worked closely with private or public leaders as a "coach"—consultant, trainer, or mentor. They think about leadership not purely for intellectual interest but with the intention of making a difference in the world.

What is Leadership?

Although the Masters approach leadership in various ways, it is striking that their thoughts have a lot in common. For example, they reach consensus on two viewpoints which respond to two major misunderstandings of leadership.

First, leadership is about activity, not about position

Leadership is something that you *exercise* or not, not something that you *have* or not. If you have exercised leadership, you are a leader; otherwise, you are not. It does not matter whether you have a splendid title or a mass of subordinates.

Jim Kouzes says that leadership is not reserved for the people at the top:

> You see "leadership" with the small "l" in every domain of life. You see leadership on the playground with kids when

someone is chosen as team leader or who emerges as a leader of a group. You see it in communities with their volunteers doing work, leading a project or leading a political activity.

Unlike managers, Kouzes says, leaders often don't have a title:

Managers tend to have a title. Leaders often do not. Managers are people who are most often appointed or selected. Leaders are people who often either emerge or might be elected. Management is a more formal operation. Leadership is often less formal. If you take some of the most recognized leaders historically—Gandhi or Martin Luther King or even, say, Mao in his early years—they weren't elected or appointed. They just led. They behaved in ways that attracted followers. So leadership is not about the title or position. It's about the behavior.

Peter Senge brings us back to the origin of the word "lead" to illuminate that leadership is an activity rather than a position:

Interestingly, "leader as boss" also deviates from the root meaning of the English verb "to lead," which comes from an Indo-European root, *leith*, "to step across a threshold." In this sense, leadership is an act of stepping ahead and of doing so in a way that can inspire others—"inspire" is another word long associated with leadership, and which appropriately means "to breathe life into." So, a deeper understanding of leadership as action versus leadership as position illuminates capacities that people have always valued: courage, which, by the way, comes from a French word meaning "tears or openings of the heart," taking risk, and bringing to life a challenging undertaking in ways that create a social field of imagination, commitment, and trust among others.

Second, leadership is about change, not about management
Warren Bennis is arguably the one who originated the saying: "Managers are people who do things right, while leaders are people

who do the right thing." Before Bennis, James MacGregor Burns distinguished between "transactional leadership" and "transformational leadership." Noel Tichy says that "transactional" is really management and "transformational" is the real leadership.

John Kotter is instrumental in replacing the term "change management" with "change leadership." He has found that a successful change initiative relies 70–90 percent on leadership, and only 10–30 percent on management. Jim Kouzes puts it this way:

> "Manage" is typically described as planning, organizing, staffing, directing, and controlling. Again, those practices have to do with keeping things in order, making sure everything is well-run and efficient.
>
> Leadership is more about movement and going places and doesn't necessarily have to do with anything being well-organized. Often it may seem chaotic and disorganized because you are trying something new or going in a new direction. Things are unknown, and the process is often messy. It's not as neat and tidy as management is often described.

Eight Disciplines of Leadership

Although there are many leitmotifs that emerge from these conversations and from the writings of the Masters, what's more remarkable is their convergence. The Masters keep hitting the same themes time and again. These are summarized below in what I call the eight *disciplines* of leadership.

I choose the word "discipline" particularly to address another misunderstanding of leadership—that it can be taught and learned in classrooms, in seminars, and/or by self-help books. Leadership cannot be taught in a leadership course or seminar. However, it can be learned, but not in classrooms or from reading self-help books. Learning is reflecting on your experience and practicing. It requires daily practice and continuing hard work. While some skills useful for leadership, such as how to make a presentation, can be taught in a workshop, I would argue, and the Masters would agree, that the foundation of leadership lies in these eight disciplines.

Discipline #1: Connecting with people

Leadership is a relationship between leaders and followers as well as an activity. Leaders must connect with followers to foster the relationship. Warren Bennis calls the relationship "a transaction between leaders and followers. Neither could exist without the other. There has to be resonance, a connection between them. So what we discovered is that leaders also *pay attention* as well as catch it."[2]

Developing trust is essential in this relationship, a point underscored by Jim Kouzes:

> Leadership is a relationship between those who aspire to lead and those who choose to follow. It is the quality of this relationship that matters most when we're engaged in getting extraordinary things done. A leader–constituent relationship that's characterized by fear and distrust will never, ever produce anything of lasting value. A relationship characterized by mutual respect and confidence will overcome the greatest adversities and leave a legacy of significance.[3]

Leaders must pay attention to the dynamics of the relationship. Howard Gardner summarizes four factors crucial to the practice of effective leadership, the first one of which he calls a tie to the community (or audience). "What needs emphasis," he says, "is that the relationship is typically ongoing, active, and dynamic."[4] So leaders must take the changing features into account.

Leaders must create a shared vision to focus this relationship. After Warren Bennis and his co-author, Burt Nanus, first published *Leaders* in 1985, the idea that leaders use a clearly articulated vision to focus people's attention has been widely embraced. However, the leader alone having the vision, and even having it shared, is not enough. Peter Senge emphasizes the idea of a shared vision, which is not the leader's vision shared by others, but a combined individual vision of all involved:

> Today, "vision" is a familiar concept in corporate leadership. But when you look carefully you find that most "visions" are one person's (or one group's) vision imposed on an

organization. Such visions, at best, command compliance—not commitment. A shared vision is a vision that many people are truly committed to, because it reflects their own personal vision.[5]

Warren Bennis, delighted to accept and apply the idea of shared vision, attributed Larry Summers' blunder during his tenure as president of Harvard University to his failure to create a shared vision among Harvard's professors and staffers although he had his personal vision. Once a university president himself, Bennis had actually made the same mistake before.

There are many reasons why a leader imposes his vision on others, and one of them might be cultural. Cho-yun Hsu, a Chinese historian, reminds us of the difference between two Golden Rules. The Western version, which was from Jesus Christ, is "Do unto others as you would have them do unto you" while the Chinese version, from the *Analects* of Confucius, is "Don't impose on others what you don't want others to impose on you." When a vision is imposed on people, particularly those who believe in the Confucian type of Golden Rule, the leadership cannot be executed effectively.

The cultural difference probably shouldn't be exaggerated here, since the importance of shared vision has been highlighted in the West too. For example, James MacGregor Burns used three quotations in the front page of *Leadership*. The first two were from Machiavelli and Franklin D. Roosevelt; the third was the following from Mao Tse-tung:

To link oneself with the masses, one must act in accordance with the needs and wishes of the masses . . . There are two principles here: one is the actual needs of the masses rather what we fancy they need, and the other is the wishes of the masses, who must make up their own minds instead of our making up their minds for them . . . We should pay close attention to the wellbeing of the masses, from the problems of land and labor to those of fuel, rice, cooking oil and salt . . . We should help them to proceed from these things to an understanding of the higher tasks which we have put forward . . . Such is the basic method of leadership.

This is a more specific version of the Confucian Golden Rule. Mao Tse-tung also offered himself as a lively example. He succeeded as a party leader and a leader of the nation when he followed the rule and failed when, later on, he betrayed it.

Connecting with people, or linking with the masses, is so essential that I list it as the first leadership discipline. It requires such skills and practices as delegation, listening, management by walking around, being generous and respectful (as Warren Bennis stresses), or even being popular (which Jim Kouzes would argue is necessary). Yet in the heart of this discipline is humanness. When Cho-yun Hsu recommends the *Analects* as reading material for Barack Obama and other leaders, and Debashis Chatterjee shares with us the story of J.R.D. Tata, their message is profoundly significant: we connect with people not only for the purpose of achieving an organizational goal, but also because they are human.

Discipline #2: Learning from failure

Leaders learn from the past, and they are particularly skillful—often through self-training and mentoring—at learning from failure. Warren Bennis detects that leaders, rather than being afraid of failure, reframe it as a valuable form of education. One of the key differences between leaders and non-leaders, he says, "is the ability of leaders to transmogrify even the negatives in their lives into something that serves them. For leaders, the uses of adversity are genuinely sweet."[6]

Bennis and, later, Bill George refer to negatives as a crucible—a life experience that transforms a person. Essential in the development of a leader, it doesn't have to be a struggle, a torture, a test, or a failure, but it is often so. And people who aspire to be leaders must have the ability to use such negatives as a transformational crucible. Since leadership is about change, or adaptive challenges that are uncertain and tough, leaders must prepare themselves for such challenges by learning from failure.

It's not enough for organizational leaders to learn from failure themselves. They must develop such a culture in their organizations. Jerry Porras quotes 3M as such an organization (you'll notice that such an example is, unfortunately, unusual):

When I teach this in executive programs, I ask the executives, "How many of you have had the opportunity to stand in front of 30 or 40 of your peers and spend one hour going into detail describing a failure you are responsible for?" Your culture may be different, but in the United States, in Western cultures, almost nobody raises their hand. In fact they laugh about it.

... At 3M the organization is structured and procedures are put in place to make these discussions happen so that someone else may learn something from it. The Post-It is a great example of someone sitting in the audience, hearing this, and figuring out there might be another application of the failed glue. And that failure became the most successful product 3M ever had.

Cho-yun Hsu comments that we tend to learn from success when we research historical cases, and that, as an example, Harvard's case-studies method is biased toward success. He talks about learning from failure from another perspective:

Success is the summation of many rational and irrational elements. You take only one chance to be successful, but you take a thousand chances to fail. So if we study leadership in history, we better study failures. They give us a lot of better lessons than studying successes.

Zizhi Tongjian ("Comprehensive Mirror in Aid for Government") is a history book from the Song Dynasty through which the writer Sima Guang and his colleagues tried to tell current leaders how past emperors and ministers succeeded or failed. The most important phrase in the book is "Guang remarks"—the author's own comments. We see more "Guang remarks" on the cases of failure than on the successes. So to me studying history is a way we learn from other people's blunders, failures, and fumbles, and try to avoid them.

Discipline #3: Reflecting on experience
Only through reflection can leaders make negatives or any other kinds of experience a valuable form of education. Otherwise, they

are only untapped resources. Warren Bennis concludes that reflection "may be the pivotal way we learn."[7] Reflection is a key to leadership emphasized by many of the Masters highlighted in this book.

Although Bennis names many ways of reflecting—including looking back, dreaming, journaling, talking it out, watching last week's game, asking for critiques, going on retreats, even telling jokes—he emphasizes one: "Having a Socratic dialog with yourself, asking the right questions at the right time, in order to discover the truth of yourself and your life. What really happened? Why did it happen? What did it do to me? What did it mean to me?"[8]

This kind of dialog with oneself is deeply rooted in Confucian traditions. The *Analects* recorded that Zengzi (or Tseng-tsu), one of the greatest disciples of Confucius, examined himself many times a day by asking such questions: "When doing things for others, have I put in my best efforts? In intercourse with friends, am I always true to my word? Have I failed to practice what I teach?"

Howard Gardner gives this discipline a special name—"getting to the mountaintop"—which underlines the importance he ascribes to reflection. It can both be literal, as in the case of Moses, and metaphorical. Gardner writes, "Periods of isolation—some daily, some extending for months or even years—are as crucial in the lives of leaders as are immersions in a crowd."[9]

Joseph Badaracco Jr. emphasizes two types of reflection:

There's also reflection in the middle of a situation, looking forward to some decision you have to make, for something you have to do. The reflection is more on what you care about, what your values are, what kind of person you are, and to some extent maybe what kind of a person you want to become. That's different from looking back simply to understand yourself. That's looking forward with the hope of shaping yourself, behaving in a certain way, living in accordance with certain values, making certain commitments. I think those are the two basic kinds of reflection that are really quite different: looking back and looking forward.

Badaracco also says that it is hard for people to practice the "looking backward" type of reflection alone: "You often need somebody else to say, 'You know, you think you are this, but you are also like that too.' Sometimes you can look back and say, 'Well, you know, that is true. I just behave that way.' So you can get a kind of self-knowledge." This "somebody" can be a leadership coach, or, as Cho-yun Hsu points out, a friend such as Franklin Roosevelt had in Colonel Howe. Or, as both Manfred Kets de Vries and Cho-yun Hsu highlight, it may be a jester (fool) as in Shakespeare's *King Lear*.

Discipline #4: Thinking deeply

Leadership tackles problems without easy answers. In many cases, the problem needs to be clearly defined first. One must identify its fundamental cause to find the real solution. As Warren Bennis and Burt Nanus summarize in *Leaders*, leadership is doing the right thing and management doing things right; leadership is about know-why and management about know-how; leadership is problem-finding and management problem-solving. Therefore, a leader must think more deeply than a manager.

Peter Senge advocates "systems thinking" in addition to personal mastery, mental models, shared vision, and team learning, which he recommends for learning organizations. A key to systems thinking is distinguishing between symptomatic solutions and fundamental solutions. A symptomatic solution that only lessens the symptoms is often preferred since it quickly achieves apparent improvements. However, since it fails to address the underlying cause, the problem may worsen. A fundamental solution often takes more time to effect, demands greater efforts, and needs people to change their behaviors and value systems, and is thus often overlooked. While it is enticing to prescribe symptomatic solutions, a leader must think deeply to discover the fundamental solution and try his best to apply it.

Howard Gardner urges leaders to think in an integrative way. He identifies four models of thinking: First, the "rigid duality" model which sees the world in terms of two opposing forces or individuals, the good and the evil; second, the "fair to a fault" model in which an individual, in considering two characters, embraces the possibility that each harbors facets of both goodness and evil; third, the "revel in relativism" model where the individual is skeptical of any perspectives; and fourth, the "personal integration" model which enables an individual to "synthesize two apparently warring sentiments: on the one hand, an awareness of the relativity of values and, on the other hand, the need to take a stance and to declare a specific position as more appropriate, at least in a given context."[10] Personal integration is the most sophisticated way of thinking, which a leader should master, but he should also be aware of and sensitive to the model of his community (audience) and address it accordingly.

Warren Bennis also discerns the value of integrative thinking, which he calls "applied creativity." This is the ability to look at a problem or crisis and see an array of unconventional solutions, or "negative capability"—the quality Keats found essential to the genius of Shakespeare:

> This gift, the poet explained in an 1817 letter to his younger brothers, is evident "when man is capable of being in uncertainties, mysteries, doubt without any irritable reaching after fact and reason." Those with negative capability may have considerable regard for fact and reason, but they also realize the wisdom of entertaining opposing views at the same time. John Gardner, for example, was able to see the past as "ballast and a teacher" and, at the same time, to realize that conventions and habits are limiting as well as comforting. "Beware," he said, "of the prisons you build to protect yourself."[11]

He observes that with this applied creativity, leaders can not only tolerate uncertainty and have the requisite hungry patience to see untested paths; but they also have the discipline necessary to achieve a desired goal.

Discipline #5: Storytelling

Leadership students are giving increasing consideration to the role of storytelling. Leadership is about change, which is best motivated when people's emotions, rather than their intellects, are touched.

Stories can touch both emotion and intellect, but are much more powerful in influencing emotions than other tools. We already have management thinkers who specialize in the subject of storytelling, among them Annette Simmons and Steve Denning. Among our Masters, besides Howard Gardner, who associates leadership exclusively with storytelling, John Kotter, Noel Tichy, and Manfred Kets de Vries all accentuate the role of storytelling in leadership.

John Kotter has practiced this craft by co-authoring a leadership fable whose characters are a group of penguins. He believes that the human brain is not built for PowerPoint slides, but for stories, and that storytelling is "a very powerful way to grab people's attention, give them an idea or two, and leave it in the brain so that it might affect their behavior . . . If it is not the most powerful tool to change behavior that can create better performance, it is certainly close."

Noel Tichy states that "the ability to create and tell certain kinds of dramatic stories is not only a useful tool, but also an essential prerequisite to being a first-class winning leader."[12] Influenced by Howard Gardner, he advocates three basic types of leadership stories. The first is the "who I am" story. Leaders use these stories to describe their fundamental views about the world and how they developed those views. The second type is the "who we are" story about the joint experiences and attitudes of the people within the organization and their shared beliefs. The third is the "where we are going" story about the future of the organization and how they are going to get there.

Gardner bases his entire thoughts of leadership on the "leaders tell stories" theme:

> I argue that the story is a basic human cognitive form; the artful creation and articulation of stories constitutes a funda-mental part of the leader's vocation. Stories speak to both parts of the human mind—its reason and emotion. And I suggest, further, that it is stories of identity—narratives that help individuals think about and feel who they are, where they come from, and where they are headed—that consti-tute the single most powerful weapon in the leader's literary arsenal."[13]

In our conversation, Gardner stresses that leaders have two challenges:

> The first challenge is coming up with the story that people pay attention to. If the story is too familiar, it just gets assimilated into the stories we already have. I almost never watch television stories because I know where they are going. They are not very interesting. On the other hand, if the story is too strange, too exotic, too eccentric, people cannot hold on to it. So the first thing the leader has to do is come up with a story which gets people's attention and makes them feel this way: "Yeah! This is very interesting. I haven't thought of this. But I can understand it."
>
> The second thing is that the story the leader tells has to be embodied in the life that the leader lives and in the way the leader behaves. If I tell one story, but in my own life I lead a very different kind of story, then in the end it doesn't have much power. I can fool people only for a while.

Manfred Kets de Vries is in agreement with Howard Gardner's sentiments when he writes:

> Effective CEOs also have to become "chief storytelling officers," inspiring people through their stories and rallying them behind their vision. As Richard Branson, one of the people the British most admire as a businessman, puts it, "All business is show business." Thus CEOs become "lead actors," setting an example (both in the daily grind and through occasional symbolic acts) that emphasizes themes they see as critical for the future of their organizations.[14]

Let me add to this a little. When a leader embodies the story consistently and sometimes dramatically, he then turns himself into a story, both metaphorically and literally. John Kotter is fond of telling the following story about Lou Gerstner: When Gerstner became CEO at IBM, the company was bureaucratic and inwardly focused. At a first divisional meeting, where managers were accustomed to presenting overhead projections, Gerstner turned off the projector and asked the managers to just talk instead. People started to tell this story at IBM, and stopped measuring success by who had the best slides. This example evidences two lessons: First, deeds speak louder than words. Second, a leadership story is most effective when it is told not by the leaders, but by people in the community where the leader tries to motivate change.

This is the old-fashioned but perennially effective "leading by example"—but in a dramatic way. The dramatization, however, whether it is deliberate or not, must be authentic. When that happens, as Howard Gardner notes, stories and embodiments can reinforce each other:

> For example, Martin Luther King, Jr.'s story about the willingness to withstand pain and criticism was exemplified in his actions. Moreover, it is a stroke of leadership genius when stories and embodiments appear to fuse, or to coalesce, as in a dream—when, as the poet William Butler Yeats would have it, one cannot tell the dancer from the dance.[15]

Discipline #6: Being a teacher

Bill George, former CEO of Medtronic and a current Harvard Business School professor, explains why leading and teaching are intertwined:

> Leadership and teaching are closely related, because as CEO you are always coaching people you work with. You try to help them become better leaders because leading a large global corporation, like I did—Medtronic now has 38,000 employees—involves developing many, many leaders. There must be hundreds of leaders throughout the company for it to be successful. And that requires that you are always coaching and helping people develop. It is less about you being a leader than developing other people to lead.

Noel Tichy would agree. While Peter Senge thinks that being a teacher is one of the leader's three roles, Tichy sees a leader's primary role as that of teacher: if you are not teaching, you are not leading. In a teaching organization, everyone teaches, everyone learns, and everyone gets smarter every day. Having worked closely with Jack Welch at GE for two years, he attributes Welch's success to being the head teacher and building GE into a teaching organization.

Being a teacher also means being a learner. It isn't only that you learn first and then teach, but that you learn through teaching. Jim Kouzes told this story from Peter Drucker:

> Peter Drucker told a story about his first manager when he was in banking. Every week his manager would sit down with him and try to teach him what he knew. Drucker said, "I'm not sure who was learning more from that, me or my manager."
>
> The best leaders are the best learners, but they are also the best teachers. They love to pass on their knowledge and experience to others. And in the process of doing so, often they learn as much. I was once asked by one of my early mentors, "What's the best way to learn something?" I thought about and I said, "To experience it, get out and try it, and see how it works." He said the best way to learn something is to teach it to somebody else. I thought: What a great observation!

James March, a master teacher, doesn't think that a teacher's task is to provide answers, or even advice. In the course of our conversation, he elaborates his views on the role of teacher:

> Teachers try to create a setting in which the student learns. I think a manager should create a setting in which workers and other managers learn. And managers should have a notion which is as hard for managers as for teachers to think: Their victories are the victories of their students, not themselves.
>
> . . . A teacher's job is to structure a world so the people see with their own eyes what they should do. I think I listen pretty well to my students, and intervene a little bit by

suggesting "Have you thought about this? Have you thought about that?"

. . . My job is not to tell people what the right answers are, but to remind them that the answer they have at the moment is not the whole answer. So I am often saying different, perhaps contradictory, things to different people.

Discipline #7: Knowing yourself

The ancient Greek aphorism "Know thyself" is as valid today as it was thousands of years ago. Warren Bennis explains that it means "separating who you are and who you want to be from what the world thinks you are and wants you to be."[16] Although he has about 30 books to his name, Bennis prefers to be addressed as the author of *On Becoming a Leader*, his favorite. Although "Know thyself" is only one chapter in that book, it is actually the foundation of becoming a leader, as Bennis emphasized at the time:

> *On Becoming a Leader* is based on the assumption that leaders are people who are able to express themselves fully. By this I mean that they know who they are, what their strengths and weaknesses are, and how to fully deploy their strengths and compensate for their weaknesses. They also know what they want, why they want it, and how to communicate what they want to others, in order to gain their cooperation and support. Finally, they know how to achieve their goals.[17]

Peter Senge argues that the first discipline of learning organizations is personal mastery. A key to personal mastery is the consciousness of personal vision, asking yourself: What do I really care about? What really matters? Leadership starts with the commitment to personal mastery.

Bill George highlights the significance of knowing yourself, or self-awareness, in *True North*: "When the 75 members of the Stanford Graduate School of Business Advisory Council were asked to recommend the most important capability for leaders to develop, their answer was nearly unanimous: self-awareness."[18] As an advocate of "Authentic Leadership," George points out that "Becoming an authentic leader is not easy. First, you have to understand yourself, because the hardest person you will ever have to lead is yourself. Once you have an understanding of your authentic self, you will find that leading others is much easier."[19]

Bill Clinton, recognized as one of the most intelligent US presidents, was not one of the most effective. A major obstacle in his way was that he didn't know himself very well. David Gergen, who worked closely with four US presidents, including Clinton, put it this way: "[M]y sense is that Clinton's central problem has been the lack of an inner compass. He has 360-degree vision but no true north. He isn't fully grounded within . . . [He] isn't exactly sure who he is yet and tries to define himself by how well others like him."[20] Howard Gardner would make a similar comment in our conversation: "Clinton is a great storyteller. He has wonderful stories. But he tells way too many, and it's not clear which one he deeply believes."

James March used to teach leadership at Stanford with *Don Quixote* as one of the teaching materials. He believes that "In some way the most important sentence in that novel is '*yo sé quien soy*,' I know who I am." Knowing yourself is a means; becoming yourself is the purpose. Bill Clinton didn't know himself well; consequently he didn't become himself well. Don Quixote, on the other hand, knows who he is; thus he becomes himself very well. Which leads us to the last leadership discipline—becoming yourself.

Discipline #8: Becoming yourself

Warren Bennis is decisive in declaring that "At bottom, becoming a leader is synonymous with becoming yourself. It's precisely that simple, and it's also that difficult."[21] To become a leader, he says, "you must become yourself, become the maker of your own life."[22] Becoming yourself has abundant and profound connotations. Let me highlight three that I deem the most significant.

First, it means to pursue your purpose and passion. As Bennis would put it to participants in his leadership course at the University of Southern California:

> Leadership is not simply like a marketing course. This is a course about life. This is a course about what you want. This

is about what your purposes are, what will give you the most happiness, impact, and benefit. Whom do you want to benefit? What kind of impact do you want? And what will make you happy and lead a good life? You're going to answer those questions. That is what this course is really about.

Purpose and passion journey together, as do being passionate and being inspirational, as Jim Kouzes has observed:

Exemplary leaders have a passion for something other than their own fame and fortune. They care about making a difference in the world. If you don't care deeply for and about something and someone, then how can you expect others to feel any sense of conviction? How can you expect others to get jazzed, if you're not energized and excited? How can you expect others to suffer through the long hours, hard work, absences from home, and personal sacrifices if you're not similarly committed?[23]

Second, it means becoming your authentic self, rather than simply imitating others. Peter Drucker, in his classic book *The Effective Executive*, noted that the effective executives he'd met didn't share any common traits. Bill George has found the same about leaders and says that "They are very, very different. Some leaders are very aggressive, and some leaders are very humble. Some leaders are brilliant, and some leaders have only average intelligence." Don't try to become Jack Welch or your boss. Become yourself and develop your unique style!

The third is the trickiest one: it means to become your "identity," or to act according to your identity. This is one of the major leadership lessons from *Don Quixote*. James March reminds us that we are living now in a world where a consequential logic dominates, where action is motivated mainly by favorable consequences, and that is exactly why the lesson from Quixote is relevant:

Quixote provides another basis for action—his sense of himself and his identity and the obligations associated with it—

a logic of appropriateness. Don Quixote creates a world in which he can live the life he considers appropriate. He draws sustenance from its correspondence with his ideals, without worrying about its consequences. He substitutes a logic of identity for a logic of reality: "I am a knight, and I shall die a knight, if so pleases the Most High."

. . . Don Quixote aims to lead a proper life—one that realizes the concept that he has of himself. He follows a logic of identity. This logic consists in acting according to one's own concept of oneself. Action is no longer justified by consequences, by what one can expect from it. We find ourselves back with Kierkegaard's assertion that a religion that can be justified (in terms of its outcomes) is no longer a religion, or with our earlier discussion about trust, love, and friendship: if they have a rational justification, then they are nothing more than economics. Human beings demonstrate their humanity not by using reason to achieve their goals, but by using their wills in defiance of reason.[24]

James March sees scandals like those of Enron and Worldcom as a consequence of what happens when accountants fail to act according to the logic of identity. While he doesn't believe that Quixote would make a good leader, Quixote illustrates "an attitude that says you don't justify great actions by expecting great things. You justify great actions because that is what is appropriate for the kind of person you are. That is a vision that has its limitations, but it is a very important thing for great leaders." March is an example himself when he says, "I think of myself as a teacher. I try to be a teacher in a Quixote sense. I try to imagine what is appropriate for a teacher and I do that."

A note of invitation

Let me conclude this Introduction with an invitation. The invitation is based on the viewpoint that leadership is about life. If we agree with Warren Bennis that becoming a leader is synonymous with becoming yourself, then we actually agree that leadership is life, or to be more accurate, as James March claims, "The fundamental issues of leadership—the complications involved in becoming, being, confronting, and evaluating leaders—are not unique to leadership. They are echoes of critical issues of life more generally."[25] In the same sense, Peter Senge is fond of quoting Confucius, "To become a leader, you must first become a human being."[26] I invite you to join us in these conversations.

Dialog is the oldest and the most effective way of learning from a master. It is no coincidence that many ancient classics, such as the *Analects* in China, the *Bhagavad Gita* in India, and the works of Plato, are of a conversational format. Therefore I have tried my best to sit down with each of the Masters to have a face-to-face conversation (making three trips to the United States to meet many and meeting some in China), and to recreate our discussions as far as possible in their original form.

There were many unforgettable moments during those conversations. One took place at Harvard Graduate School of Education in October 2008, when I was able to talk with both Howard Gardner and Peter Senge. (Senge requested to join us when he heard that I would interview Gardner, whom he admires.) On a list of influential business thinkers, published in the *Wall Street Journal* earlier that year, Gardner was ranked # 5 and Senge # 11. The conversation was truly exciting.

Gardner was excited about the news he'd read earlier that the Chinese Premier Wen Jiabao was reading Marcus Aurelius, commenting "It is a name probably not many people in this building would know. It is like George Bush saying he was reading the *Analects* of Confucius."

I pointed out that *Meditations* by Marcus Aurelius had sold very well in China since Wen Jiabao revealed that he had read the book more than a hundred times. "But you know," I added, "it has probably still sold less than *The Fifth Discipline*, which has sold about one million copies in China."

Senge, the author of *The Fifth Discipline*, responded: "The success of the book was a mixed blessing. There has been a big problem in China: the book is meant to help people do things, but there is a huge gap between superficial awareness and practical experience."

Wen Jiabao didn't make his message clear, which I suppose is: Don't just read *Meditations*—Meditate! Yet Peter Senge's message is clear: Don't read *The Fifth Discipline*—Practice it!

While I'm determined to present this book in a conversational format, I don't only want to invite you to join in these dialogs. More importantly, I would like you to use them as an instrument for reflection and action. Let me make my invitation clear: Don't just read. For the purpose of becoming a leader—and becoming a human being first—join in these conversations, reflect upon your experience, and act on these disciplines!

Endnotes

1 James MacGregor Burns, *Leadership* (Harper & Row, 1978), 2.

2 Warren Bennis and Burt Nanus, *Leaders: Strategies for Taking Charge* (Collins Business Essentials, 2007), 30.

3 Jim Kouzes and Barry Posner, *The Leadership Challenge* (Jossey-Bass, 2007), 24.

4 Howard Gardner, *Leading Minds* (Basic Books, 1996), 36.

5 Peter Senge, *The Fifth Discipline: The Art & Practice of the Learning Organization* (Doubleday, 2006), 192.

6 Warren Bennis and Robert Thomas, *Leading for a Lifetime* (Harvard Business School Press, 2007), 18.

7 Warren Bennis, *On Becoming a Leader* (Basic Books, 2003), 106–07.

8 Ibid., 54.

9 Gardner, op. cit., 36.

10 Ibid., 45.

11 Bennis and Thomas, op. cit., 101.

12 Noel Tichy with Eli Cohen, *The Leadership Engine* (Collins Business Essentials, 2005), 217–18.

13 Gardner, op. cit., 43.

14 Manfred Kets de Vries, *The Leadership Mystique: Leading Behavior in the Human Enterprise* (Prentice Hall, 2006), 55.

15 Gardner, op. cit., 37.

16 Bennis, op. cit., 48.

17 Ibid., xxvii.

18 Bill George with Peter Sims, *True North: Discover Your Authentic Leadership* (Jossey-Bass, 2007), 69.

19 Ibid., xxxiii.
20 Ibid., xx.
21 Bennis, op. cit., xxxiii.
22 Ibid., 46.
23 Kouzes and Posner, op. cit., 116.
24 James March and Thierry Weil, *On Leadership* (Blackwell Publishing, 2005), 85–86.
25 Ibid., 1.
26 Senge, op. cit., 318.

Essential Leadership Qualities

CHAPTER 1

Jim Kouzes: Leadership is Everybody's Business

Jim Kouzes is the co-author, with Barry Posner, of *The Leadership Challenge*, one of the most influential leadership books, which is currently in its fourth edition. He is the Dean's Executive Professor of Leadership at the Leavey School of Business of Santa Clara University (SCU). He served as president, then CEO and chairman of the Tom Peters Company from 1988 to 2000, and directed the Executive Development Center at SCU from 1981 to 1987. The *Wall Street Journal* has cited him as one of the 12 best executive educators in the US.

Jim Kouzes traces his interest in leadership back to January 20, 1961, when he served in John F. Kennedy's Honor Guard at the Presidential Inauguration as one of only a dozen Eagle Scouts. But it wasn't until 1982 when he joined the staff at SCU that he, together with SCU professor Barry Posner, began to dedicate himself to serious research on the practice of leadership.

Kouzes and Posner became intrigued by what people did when they were exercising leadership at their best. They asked leaders across all types of organizations to tell them Personal Best Leadership stories, and they have been asking the same question since. Based on their research, they wrote *The Leadership Challenge*, first published in 1987, and presented The Five Practices of Exemplary Leadership (which is a registered trademark of Kouzes and Posner):

(1) Model the Way, (2) Inspire a Shared Vision, (3) Challenge the Process, (4) Enable Others to Act, and (5) Encourage the Heart.

After more than 25 years' continuous research, Kouzes and Posner maintain that the five practices are enduring and universal. In the preface to the fourth edition of *The Leadership Challenge* released in 2007, they write: "Nothing in our continuing research has told us that there is a magical sixth practice that will revolutionize the conduct of leadership, and nothing in our research suggests that any of the Five Practices are now irrelevant."

With over 1.8 million copies sold and available in 22 languages, *The Leadership Challenge* is a bestseller around the world, including China. The appeal comes from its lucid structure: Leadership is about doing five things—and it comes with a guarantee. Kouzes and Posner write, "We also make you a promise: everything in this book is evidence-based. Everything we write about, everything we advise is solidly based in research—our own and others. If you engage in the practices we describe in this book, you will improve your perform-ance and the performance of your team."

While this sounds simple enough, simple does not mean easy. For example, in a marathon you need to complete 42 kilometers, which is quite simple but not easy at all. Having this clearly in mind, Kouzes and Posner offered this caveat: "There is a catch, of course. You have to do it with commitment and consistency. Excellence in anything—whether it's leadership, music, sports, or engineering—requires disciplined practice."

The Leadership Challenge is not only a book. Kouzes and Posner have created other products around it and also over a dozen other books. What is intriguing is that they always do it together as co-authors. Kouzes–Posner is not a co-brand, but a single brand. When I requested an interview with Kouzes, he recommended a three-way conversation together with "Barry." Regrettably, when I visited Kouzes, Posner was busy with other commitments.

Unlike Posner, who has remained at SCU, Kouzes left acade-mia for a while to run the Tom Peters Group Learning Systems in 1988 as president of the consultancy, and later on, CEO and chairman of the Tom Peters Company until 2000 (a role he refers to as that of a player/coach). Having come back to SCU as the Dean's Executive Professor of Leadership, Kouzes is now more of a coach.

Expertise and experience aside, Kouzes is also a considerate coach. When I talked to him in San Francisco in June 2008, a month after a massive earthquake hit the province of Sichuan in China, he opened the conversation by asking whether the earthquake had affected any of my family. He also showed his thoughtfulness in the way that he had meticulously prepared notes for the list of questions I had submitted earlier. Even before we started our dialog, Kouzes was already modeling the way.

Leadership is about Ordinary People

Liu: In the preface of *The Leadership Challenge*, it says that the book is about how ordinary people exercise leadership at their best. By ordinary people, I think you mean people who are not in a very obvious, or very high, leadership position. So what does leadership mean to ordinary people?

Kouzes: Our work has been based on an assumption that leadership is not reserved for the people at the top. It's not reserved for people who are elected officials. It's not reserved for people who are military generals. It's not reserved for people of any political status. You see "leadership" with the small "l" in every domain of life.

You see leadership on the playground with kids when someone is chosen as team leader or who emerges as a leader of a group. You see it in communities with their volunteers doing work, leading a project or leading a political activity.

You see leadership at home. In fact, the most important leadership role model for 18–30-year-olds, according to the research that Barry and I did, comes from family members, followed by teachers and coaches, then followed by community leaders, and, only after that, business leaders.

So it's pretty apparent that leadership is not just something about people who are CEOs and those who make the cover of magazines. It is something that is not dependent on age, gender, or position. Leadership is something everyone can do.

Although we have interviewed many CEOs, what we wanted to know is not what CEOs do that makes them the most effective. We also wanted to know what made people who were in any leadership roles, regardless of level, effective.

So we decided to construct a research project that asked people from supervisor level all the way up to the very top of organizations. Given the nature of our study, the majority were middle managers. After the first edition of *The Leadership Challenge* we expanded our study to include student leaders, as well as others outside of formal organizations. We asked: What is it that you are doing when you are performing at your best as a leader? We collected hundreds of Personal Best stories, and we literally took three-by-five cards and wrote down the specific behaviors from both the interviews and written cases that described what leaders did when at their best. We then organized these and it became our Five Practices.

If you are going to learn about leadership that is not based on a position, you need to study people who are across the range of leadership roles. The best way to do that is by asking them to tell a story about their best experience as a leader. If you do enough of that, you find enough people agreeing on certain things, and common themes become apparent. So like any initial observational research, that's what we did. The Five Practices of Exemplary Leadership emerged from our analysis of the hundreds of cases and interviews.

Later, we tested the validity and reliability of our findings using an assessment questionnaire, The Leadership Practices Inventory (LPI), that measured the extent to which leaders engaged in The Five Practices and the impact these behaviors had on the attitudes and performance of team members. In addition to our research, after 25 years, more than 400 doctoral studies have been done using this model in a variety of different settings, testing its validity and its reliability. Ours is one of the most rigorously tested leadership models in use today.

Leadership is about Movement

Liu: Would you like to give a definition of leadership?

Kouzes: In our book, we define leadership as the art of mobilizing others to want to struggle for shared aspirations. And each of those words is chosen very carefully.

It is an "art" because even though we have tried to put some science to leadership—if leaders do certain things they will have these outcomes, and we do our best as researchers to validate this—there is a lot you can't account for. There is a lot that comes from the person, the person's style, and the person's background. There's also the culture of the company and the country, the industry, the state of the economy, and a host of other variables. Leadership is very much like a performing art, because you are doing it with other people or in front of other people. It's not something you do on your own. It's not an art like painting.

It is about "mobilizing others" because leadership is about movement. If you look up "manage" and "lead" in a dictionary, you'll find that "manage" comes from the word "manus" which means "hand." Being a manager is about essentially handling things, organizing and making sure everything is in good shape, and being efficient—those kinds of connotations. The origin of the word "lead" comes from the words "go," "travel," and "guide." Leadership is about going places. So you are mobilizing others.

We use "want to" because people do their best only when they do things of their own volition and when they are personally committed. People who do it because they have to do it, because they are getting a paycheck, because they are afraid they will be punished by their manager, or because they are told to do it, do not produce the best outcome. So there is an element of making sure that people want to do this, not just have to do this.

And it is a "struggle." Leadership is often presented as too easy: here is the formula, do these five things, and you should be successful. But in fact it's all about hard work, difficulty, adversity, and challenge.

And last, leadership is about "shared aspirations" because it is not about the leader's vision and values, it is about the collective. A leader represents a group of people, or represents a cause with a set of principles, not just himself or herself.

All of these are important elements of this definition. It's also consistent with the origin, which is to "go," "travel," and "guide," a sense of going someplace.

Managers must be Leaders

Liu: You have touched on the difference between leadership and management. Probably in many people's minds, leadership is a better thing than management. What is your response to that?

Kouzes: Well, I had a manager title after my name for much of my career. My father had a manager title after his name. Managers tend to have a title. Leaders often do not. Managers are people who are most often appointed or selected. Leaders are people who often either emerge or might be elected. Management is a more formal operation. Leadership is often less formal. If you take some of the most recognized leaders historically—Mahatma Gandhi or Martin Luther King or even, say, Mao in his early years—they weren't elected or appointed. They just led. They behaved in ways that attracted followers. So leadership is not about the title or position. It's about the behavior.

There is a distinction between "manage" and "lead" based on their word origins and the way the functions are typically described. "Manage" is typically described as planning, organizing, staffing, directing, and controlling. Again, those practices have to do with keeping things in order, making sure everything is well-run and efficient.

Leadership is more about movement and going places and doesn't necessarily have to do with anything being well organized. Often it may seem chaotic and disorganized because you are trying something new or going in a new direction. Things are unknown, and the process is often messy. It's not as neat and tidy as management is often described.

That said, while there is a distinction between the two, we don't find it necessarily very useful to make a big deal out of it. We try not to in our book because a manager—a person with a title—also has to be a leader. In today's environment people expect both, not just one or the other. Managers must manage, and they must lead.

Now the same is not true for leaders. Leaders don't always have to be managers. Again take the example of some of the most famous historical leaders of movements; they are not necessarily people with formal titles and they don't have the expectation that they'll do all the things that managers do, like make a budget or do a plan. But they are expected to provide some sense of direction, and some sense that we can all do this together, the things we expect from leaders.

Peter Drucker once said that he thought this was false dichotomy because the person who is expected to lead and manage is the same person. You can't really cut the person in half and say this half is a manager, and that half is a leader. You are both.

Leadership is about Popularity

Liu: I read your recent blog where you said maybe leadership is a popularity test. Peter Drucker has said that leadership is not about being popular. Could you elaborate on this?

Kouzes: Barry and I once wrote an essay called "Leaders Should Want to be Liked." I also wrote that blog after I happened to arrive in downtown San Francisco on the day that the torch was being carried through the streets of San Francisco for the Beijing Olympics.

It just struck me as I followed the news reports several days after, how a leader, Gavin Newsom, the mayor in this particular case, was being criticized from all sides. It's like nothing he could do was the right thing because if he took one action, he would have upset the people who were protesting, and if he took another action, he would have upset those who were carrying the torch and those who were sponsoring it. It's one of the classical lose-lose situations. Yet as much as that was true, as mayor he still had to maintain support.

This experience caused me to reflect on something you'll hear some leaders often say: "I don't care if people like me; I just want them to respect me." I don't know if you have a similar kind of phrase in Chinese, but it's something you will often hear in English.

Do they really mean that? Are the people who say this truly serious about not wanting others to like them? And who is the "they" leaders are talking about when they make that statement? Can they really mean that they don't care if their spouses don't like them, or their kids don't like them, or their business partners don't like them, or their employees don't like them, or their friends (would they have any?) don't like them?

I think this is just an excuse for bad, self-protective behavior. If those leaders really do believe that, then they are limiting their capacity to get extraordinary things done. Our data show that when people say they like their manager, their effectiveness is higher, their performance is higher, and their satisfaction with the organization is also higher. If it's true that people will perform at higher levels if they like you, then you should want to be liked. It's no different from saying: if I set goals, people are more likely to perform at higher levels, therefore I should set goals. There is no difference between those two statements.

Then why do they say "I don't care if people like me; I just want them to respect me"? Frankly I think it's because many leaders need an excuse for doing things that are not likeable. But it's not unlike being a parent. Do you have kids?

Liu: Yes, I have two sons.

Kouzes: So you know that sometimes, in the best interest of your children, you have to do things they may not like. It comes with being a parent. When you do something that they don't like, your kids may even say out of anger "I hate you, Dad." (We know they really don't mean it, because they're upset at the moment. It passes pretty quickly, and they are fine the next minute.) It's a very similar situation when you're in the leader role.

We often have to make decisions as leaders that other people do not agree with and do not like. That doesn't mean that we have to make those decisions or take those actions in a manner that causes people not to like us. We can do it in such a way that at the end of the day others will still say, on the scale of "dislike" to "like," that they like us as leaders. We perform in such a way that makes them like us.

Leadership is a relationship. If people have a more positive feeling about their leader, they are much more likely to perform at higher levels. Isn't that their job, anyway? Leaders are here to improve performance, not to diminish it. That said, neither Gavin Newsom in San Francisco nor any leader in any country, in any company, in any governmental agency or not-for-profit organization will ever be liked by 100 percent of people. That's an impossibility.

Liu: There was an article in the *Harvard Business Review* called "The Great Intimidators," which argued that fear is also a great motivator.

Kouzes: What we know about fear is that physiologically it causes the kinds of responses that shut the body down. If you become fearful, you become much more vigilant, you are always watching out, you become much more self-protective and much more interested in yourself rather than in the broader community and what happens to others. This is all very physiological. Your blood goes to your basic organs, you are there ready to fight and protect, but you are not there to create, to take big risks and things like that.

So fear may be effective as an emotion if you want people to stop being effective. But if you want people to take risks, perform at higher levels, be innovative, and also enjoy what they are doing, then fear is not the emotion you want to instill. Intimidation may get people to do things but it definitely does not get them to do their best. That's really the important thing to remember.

Leaders are also Followers

Liu: When I first received an email from you, I noticed your signature line "love 'em and lead 'em." I love that, particularly the first part, "love them." But I'm a little concerned about the second part.

As you said, leadership is a relationship between leaders and followers. I think we are not only leaders, but also followers in many more situations. So, do we over-emphasize leadership compared with what we might call "followership?"

Kouzes: It is a great question. We haven't actually done as much research on "followership," but all leaders are also followers, except perhaps for the chairman of the board. Even that person has to respond to the shareholders in a capitalist system, or has to respond to some other higher authority; so even those at the top are following somebody. Just like manager/leader in many respects is a false dichotomy, leader/follower is a false dichotomy because we can all be both.

A middle manager is a classic example. A middle manager has to lead those who, in a hierarchical system, report to him or her, but also follow the direction that comes from above. We are often caught up in thinking "Well, I can't behave in ways that are other than what I'm told to do from the top, so I just have to cascade those orders down to the bottom" in the very classical, rigid, militaristic, or bureaucratic sense. But if I look at myself both as a leader and a follower, I have some choices to make along the way.

I can choose to say: "This is aligned with the values we all agree on. This is aligned with the purpose, with the organization, and I am choosing to follow." On the other hand I might come to a different conclusion and say: "You know, while this is one way of making this company effective, I have an innovative and creative idea that I think will make us even more effective. It is consistent with our organizational vision and values. But it is not one that people who are above me are advocating. I'm going to take the risk and put that idea forward in a way that will enlist them in it." And when I do that, I'm becoming the leader.

I'll tell you a little story. It's a classical example. I think it is still included in the fourth edition of *The Leadership Challenge.* When Gail Mayville worked for Ben & Jerry's Ice Cream, the ice cream manufacturer in Vermont, she heard they had a problem. At the time, she was an administrative assistant. She didn't have a title as a manager. Everyone was essentially her boss and she was at the bottom of the ladder, at the bottom of the hierarchy. But she had an idea on what would be valuable for the company to do to solve a critical problem. So when she decided that she would present that idea, she moved into the role of being a leader. So people can lead from any position. You don't have to be the CEO. You don't have to be a middle manager. You can be in both roles at the same time.

We are both leaders and followers. Sometimes we do our best to make sure that we enthusiastically implement what everyone has agreed on. Other times when I have an innovative and different way of doing something, let me put on my "leader hat" and try to put it forward, inspire a vision of the future and enlist other people.

Asians are more Forward-Looking

Liu: Have you been to China?

Kouzes: Twice.

Liu: Do you feel Chinese managers are different from managers in other places?

Kouzes: I can answer that in two ways.

First, if you look at our data, they do not show any meaningful differences. There may be some statistically significant differences, but not meaningful differences. For example, based on the scores on our *Leadership Practices Inventory*—our leader assessment instrument—it looks like Americans are better leaders than Asians. That is, American leaders score higher on most of the practices compared to Asian leaders. But we think that is not the case. We think it's a case of how people view the scale.

There is a tendency among Asian people when responding to this kind of survey to give a lower number rather than a higher number. Given a choice between giving someone a 7 and an 8, Asians will tend to give a 7 while Americans will tend to give an 8. We call it grade inflation in education. Americans seem to have a slightly more positive view of themselves, but it doesn't mean they are actually better.

That's why we don't look at the absolute scores so much as whether the lines are parallel to each other. They are; meaning Asians and Americans look very similar in terms of the leadership practices on which they score high, moderate and low. Essentially this means that we are relatively similar in our practices. This is also true across other cultures. This tells us that there are some leadership universals. There are some universal practices that work.

Liu: There is a table in *The Leadership Challenge* showing the selection of people from different countries for the most admired leadership qualities. China is not in the table, but it illustrates the difference between other Asian countries and North America.

In the top four qualities, the Japanese and Koreans rank "Forward-looking" first, and "Inspiring" last. But the Canadians and Americans rank "Honest" first and "Competent" last.

Kouzes: Among all qualities, only "Honest," "Forward-looking," "Inspiring" and "Competent" get more than 60 percent universally. Their relative ranking may be different, but these are the only four leader qualities that 60 percent or more of people around the world say they look for in leaders. These four qualities make a composite picture of what we *most* expect of leaders. This is as true today as it was when we first started doing our research.

It is also true that in Asia there is a tendency to value "Forward-looking" more than any of these other qualities, which reinforces the point that being forward-looking is the one quality that differentiates leaders from other credible people, which we report in another book, *Credibility*. By the way, in addition to doing the research on what people look for in their leaders, we also did research on what people looked for in a colleague. We used the same list of attributes so we could compare the results. It was most intriguing to find that "forward-looking" was not something that the majority of people looked for in a colleague, but 71 percent of people looked for this quality in a leader.

And we are willing to acknowledge that in Asia the thinking is longer-term. People may often make the observations that we think short-term in the United States. There is much truth in this. We are so driven by numbers, quotas, and results that we lose sight of the long term. In America, we expect leaders to think long-term, but the pressures of business force them to think short-term.

Liu: There is another observation that stands out. Asian people don't expect the manager or the leader to be as "inspiring" as many people in the United States do. That's a very interesting finding.

Kouzes: That is another distinction that we would acknowledge. The classic example is perhaps the sales person—always upbeat, positive, like a cheerleader. In Asia, you don't see that kind of behavior. That's cultural. Nevertheless, the expectation to be inspiring is held by more than 50 percent in many Asian countries; it's just that it is not as strong as it is in the West.

The Humility Factor

Liu: Let's talk about humility a little bit. In *The Leadership Challenge*, you say: "Humility is the only way to resolve the conflicts and contradictions of leadership." After reading that statement, I have two questions. First, how do you define humility? Second, are leaders like Bill Gates and Steve Jobs humble?

Kouzes: I love to look up the meaning of a word when I don't understand it. I don't just look up the definition, I look up the origin. "Humility" comes from a word that I think originally comes from an Arabic word, "humus," meaning "earth."

When I think about "humility," I think "down-to-earth." We often think about leaders as being at the very top. They get the suite on the top floor of the building. They are at the top of the hierarchy. Leaders who have humility may have the position that puts them in a very senior rank of the organization, but they don't ever forget where they came from, where they started. They don't ever lose touch with the people on the ground floor. They understand that if it weren't for those people, they wouldn't be where they are. So they don't flaunt their wealth, they don't abuse their status; they hardly ever talk about it.

To me, the best example of someone who is not humble is Donald Trump. He has put his name on all of his buildings. You know he is a TV star. He dresses like he is better than the rest. He arrives in limousines and all of those things say: "You know I am not you. And I'm proud of it."

The best leaders don't take that kind of attitude. They acknowledge that if it weren't for the people who show up every day and work really hard, this organization wouldn't be as effective as it is. It's not about me, it's about us. People may say it's the CEO who does this, the CEO who does that. But it's really not the case. It's a team of people that makes that possible. We reinforce this notion that leaders are people who are part of us, not above us.

And yes, Steve Jobs and Bill Gates, as well as Michael Dell, and Richard Branson, these iconic figures in business are not very humble people, and their organizations have been effective. But there are also Gandhi, other political or religious leaders, and people we write about in our book. In business, Warren Buffet is someone who is also thought of as a very humble person. Unlike Steve Jobs, these are people who don't put themselves above others.

Liu: So you would take Steve Jobs as an exception to the rule.

Kouzes: I would say that Steve Jobs is an exception to the rule if you look at leadership in its broadest sense. However, Steve Jobs probably is not an exception if you take leaders of the Fortune 100 or Fortune 500 companies.

Leaders are Teachers and Learners

Liu: In *The Leadership Challenge* you say, "Leaders try, fail, learn. That's the leaders' mantra. Leaders are learners." I agree with you that leaders are learners. A lot of people are also saying leaders are teachers. What do you think about that?

Kouzes: Peter Drucker told a story about his first manager when he was in banking. Every week his manager would sit down with him and try to teach him what he knew. Drucker said, "I'm not sure who was learning more from that, me or my manager."

The best leaders are the best learners, but they are also the best teachers. They love to pass on their knowledge and experience to others. In the process of doing so, often they learn as much. I was once asked by one of my early mentors, "What's the best way to learn something?" I thought about and I said, "To experience it, get out and try it, and see how it works." He said the best way to learn something is to teach it to somebody else. I thought: What a great observation!

That is not as easy as it sounds. Those who are teaching others, who are the best at it, are constantly learning things themselves. I find that when I have to prepare for, say, a new client, I'm doing a lot of reading and studying, asking a lot of questions and interviewing people to make sure that I have a better understanding of that particular client. I always love what I do because I am always learning. I love learning.

I think the two are in a sense the opposite sides of the same coin. If I am going to be a good teacher of others, I need to be a good learner.

The observation that leaders are learners also came from research that we did. Again it is those leaders who engage more frequently in learning who are more likely to be effective than those who engage less often in learning; which makes sense since practice is important. It takes more practice to become an exemplary leader than it does to become an ordinary leader.

Liu: Practice does not necessarily lead to knowledge. I mean practice per se. You have to reflect. Practice plus reflection, then you learn.

Kouzes: Becoming the best at anything requires essentially four things: having a particular goal to improve in some way; having a method for learning that and achieving that; having feedback about how well you are doing; and also paying as much attention to the method as to the outcome because we don't always get the outcome we would like the first time we try something. So if you are doing all those things you are deliberately practicing and learning continuously. And leaders can do that.

One of the things I often say is that it takes at least two hours of practice every day to stay the same; more if you want to get better. Most leaders respond by saying, "But I don't have two hours a day to add to my day. I'm already working hard." I say it's not that you have to add it but you have to use your time differently. You can structure your time in such a way that it might be 15 minutes here and 15 minutes there, and you are looking at it as a learner, which means you are stepping back and reflecting. "I wanted this result. And I was trying to do it this way. How well did I do it? Did I get the result? What went right? What went wrong? What can I do differently? Let me try something again." If you look at it that way, then you are practicing.

Preaching and Practice

Liu: Both you and Dr. Posner hold or have held leadership positions in an organization. How was your experience of walking the talk, practicing what you preach? Did you find it different? Was it exciting or disappointing?

Kouzes: In some respects my role model for leading was my father. One of the things I noticed about my dad was that he was always going to school, and he was always trying to teach as well. One of the things I always remember in growing up was how much I admired his ability to handle all of that.

So my own experience with leading, I think, contributes a lot to the realness because for every practice, every recommendation, the test for me was, "Could I do this? Could I apply this to the work that I do? Or is this totally some theoretical notion that is not practical, not applicable?" So in my case, being a manager in an educational institution and being a CEO of a consulting company enabled me to get a reality test. Barry will tell you the same is true for him. He was the dean of the Leavey School of Business at SCU for 12 years. He knows what it's like to try to put into practice the things that we write about.

He and I also say that applying this is harder than writing about it, because in writing about it you are simply talking about the ideal situation, about how it ought to be. But when you are dealing with real people in real-life situations, there's often a difference between intention and execution. I think about it in terms of my golf game. I love to read golf magazines and imagine myself doing all those things that the pros recommend. But there's a difference between reading an article about golf and actually going out and playing golf. It's not as easy as it looks in those pictures. Barry and I are the first to say that leadership is a struggle. There's always a struggle going on. There are always conflicts.

Still, writing about leadership helped us both be better leaders, and being leaders helped us be better researchers and writers.

Liu: You mentioned that writing about leadership might be easier than practicing leadership. I don't necessarily agree with you. It's probably just different. Writing as thorough and thoughtful a book as *The Leadership Challenge* is pretty difficult.

Kouzes: Yes, it is. It's now in its fourth edition. The first edition was about a year-long research project, a year-long writing project, and another year of all the editing back and forth. You are right. It's just different.

Liu: Warren Bennis used to be president of a university. After that, he said he finally realized he preferred more to be a coach than to be a player. Which role do you prefer, coach or player?

Kouzes: I really wanted to be a player/coach for most of my career. I wanted to both coach and play. I knew that I really liked teaching and I liked engaging other managers who were struggling with the same issues, and coaching and teaching. Currently in this stage of my life, I prefer to be a coach, not a player/coach.

Liu: My last question is about this Kouzes–Posner co-brand. It's amazing, you know. Co-authorship is fairly common but a long-lasting co-authorship is very, very unusual. How are you able to make it work?

Kouzes: You are right. It is very unusual. There are a couple of keys to our success, I believe.

First of all, Barry and I have a passion for our subject matter. We met because we had this common interest. And neither one of us seems to have the personality that wants to be dominant over the other. We are quite collaborative, willing to let one take the lead on something and the other one take the follower role, and vice versa.

Another key is that Barry had his role in another setting that was different from mine. So we were never like academic colleagues competing for tenure in the same institution, or we weren't working in the same consulting firm and both trying to run the company. That might have created conflicts.

When we collaborate on a book, it's pretty much a 50:50 proposition: he writes half, I write half. If it is a project where it may be appropriate for one to do more than the other, we are able to make sure that there is another project where the roles are reversed. I think this has served us well.

Liu: But your name always comes first.

Kouzes: Yes, except on some articles. I think the first time we did it the decision was ultimately based on age. I'm older. Age has its privileges sometimes, and I suppose this is one of them.

CHAPTER

Warren Bennis: Generous Leadership

Warren Bennis is University Professor and Distinguished Professor of Business Administration and Founding Chairman of The Leadership Institute at the University of Southern California. He has written or edited some 30 books, including the bestselling *Leaders* and *On Becoming a Leader*, both translated into 21 languages. The *Wall Street Journal* named him as one of the top 10 speakers on management in 1993 and in 1996. *Forbes* magazine has referred to him as the "Dean of Leadership Gurus."

This most famous and respected of leadership gurus—and the only one with real experience of leading a large organization—has in his time taught other luminaries such as Charles Handy; has acted as consultant to four US presidents; and was one of the youngest infantry officers on the European front in the Second World War.

However, when I met this short, amiable elder, he did not consciously carry these various auras with him into our conversation—although they shone, sometimes spontaneously. Rather, he brought to it a very youthful heart. He perfectly epitomized "neoteny," a term from the field of biology referring to the retention of juvenile characteristics into adulthood, which he had used to describe elder leaders in his book *Geeks and Geezers*. Or in Chinese tradition, he had *chizi zhi xin*, "a heart of a newborn baby."

It is hard to believe that the man I met in May 2008 was an 83-year-old with a lifetime of accomplishments behind him. He had just finished his regular workout when he arrived for our appointment in a hotel near the beautiful beach of Santa Monica, California. If he is youthful in appearance, he is more so at heart. Though he has authored or co-authored so many books, he talked passionately about his next three! He regretted that he knew little about China and was hoping for some recommendations about Confucius from me.

In a word, Bennis is still looking forward with a heart of a new-born baby.

A Generalist with a Leadership Brand

Liu: How do you like the word "guru?"

Bennis: It's overused. I once heard someone say that people who use "guru" don't know how to spell . . .

Liu: . . . charlatan?

Bennis: You heard that. That's the reason I think some people reject the word "guru." But it is a big compliment to be called a guru. It really means you show the light, to use its Hindu meaning. However, it is used rather indiscriminately.

Liu: You said Charles Handy [a former student of Bennis's] thinks of himself as a philosopher.

Bennis: He is, actually. If you asked Charles, "Do you like to be called a management guru?" I could predict his answer.

Liu: How do you think of yourself? Philosopher? Thinker?

Bennis: Me? I think I am more of a generalist.

Liu: A fox, as you've described it [see box].

Bennis: Yes, very much. My career's been very long. I have been active, you know, more than half a century. I wrote my first article in 1954. My first book, which was co-authored, was published in 1961. It was called *The Planning of Change*, which was almost arrogantly titled, saying that you could plan change in a world with such turbulence and chaos. More recently I've been "branded" as a leadership guru. I prefer not being a "brand."

The Fox and the Hedgehog

Originating in a fragment attributed to the Greek poet Archilochus, and elaborated by the British philosopher Isaiah Berlin, the metaphor of the fox and the hedgehog refers to two kinds of intellectuals. Foxes, such as Aristotle, Shakespeare and Goethe, know many things, pursue various ends at the same time and see the world in all its complexity, but never integrate their thinking into one overall concept. Hedgehogs, such as Plato, Nietzsche and Proust, on the contrary, know one big thing and simplify a complex world into a basic idea that unifies everything.

Among the leadership authors included in this book, Warren Bennis and Howard Gardner have written explicitly about the contrast. Bennis has a balanced view of the two: "Hedgehogs, at their best, produce Darwins; at their worst, pedants. Foxes occasionally can claim an Einstein or an Oppenheimer but more often are dilettantes." Intriguingly, both Bennis and Gardner think of themselves as foxes and share a secret admiration for the hedgehog. Bennis wrote, "I'm clearly a fox with a sneaking admiration for the hedgehog," while Gardner admitted, "I am a fox that would like to be a hedgehog."

An Old Dog with New Tricks

Liu: I know you are writing poetry now. Will you publish, as James March does?

Bennis: I have published some poems, back in 1979 during a hospital stay in London. But I still want to write a play. I've got three more books in mind right now which I want to tell you about. None of these has been started, so I haven't actually framed them yet.

One of them will be what the publisher would like to call *A Warren Bennis Reader*. But I don't think that will be the final title.

Liu: Something like *The Essential Warren Bennis*, perhaps?[1]

Bennis: I am not sure of this yet, because there are two ways I can go about it. One is simply a collection of some of my favorite writings.

Liu: I think you have done that in *Managing the Dream*.

Bennis: *Managing the Dream* has some of them, but there has been a lot more since then. And I want to redo it.

The other way would be to do it as a leadership course, because I think a lot of people would like a textbook on how to teach leadership. So it could have a number of my articles, but articles by other people as well. It could be both a textbook and a book of readings. It'll be very difficult to do, but it might be more appealing and more useful.

The second book, which my publisher is very keen on, is something I refer to as Project X.[2] It's not going to be an autobiography; it's not going to be a memoir; it's not going to be a diary—but it's going to be a way of using my life experiences to write about leadership and life. So it's going to be a series of essays which will capture many of the issues that the leadership literature tends to ignore or avoid: issues like envy, ambition, death, loss, sex, greed, and love.

The third book I want to do is a small book I am going to call *Generous Company*. It's about the significance in leadership and life of being magnanimous, being generous, and giving back to others. This is an area not written about, but it is the key to leadership and organizational lives.

The New Crucible and an Old Epiphany

Liu: In *True North*, Bill George wrote about crucibles and epiphany. He told me that he got the idea from you. But it seems to me that you don't write enough about your own crucibles and your own epiphany.

Bennis: It is true the only crucible of my own I used in my book was about my growing up in a family during the Depression. But we continue to have crucibles if we keep learning. There's not just one. For example, the most exciting, difficult crucible for me right now is becoming old. It is scary and exciting. There is no preparation for it. How do you prepare to become old? It's an adventure, and I try very hard to do it wisely and to learn from that.

Liu: A question Paul Ylvisaker asked you proved to be an epiphany to you, didn't it?

Bennis: When I was at Harvard giving a talk in 1977, Paul asked me, "Do you really love being president of the University of Cincinnati?" That was a turning point for me because I realized that I did not love what I was doing. The beauty of that story is that I was a hostage to my role model. I realized that was not where my passion was. It wasn't quite inauthentic. I wasn't being an impostor. But I wasn't doing something that I really loved.

When Paul Ylvisaker asked the question, I realized I was trying to be Dr. Douglas McGregor, who was my mentor. I said to myself: "No, let's stop. I am not enjoying this. I enjoy writing and teaching." I knew I could be OK as university president, but I knew also that it wasn't my passion.

Five Leadership Qualities

Liu: When you told that story in *Managing the Dream*, you said you found one thing in common in great leaders: they love their job. And in *Leaders*, the book you co-authored with Burt Nanus, you said that when you asked all those leaders what enabled them to do their job, they talked about one thing: learning.

Bennis: Curiosity.

Liu: That's a question I'm going to ask. You talk about how those great leaders share some common traits. However, in different cases, you name different traits. Sometimes you say passion, and sometimes you say learning. Sometimes you say something else. So what are those common traits or characteristics those great leaders share?

Bennis: [Laughs] I'll name five that I think stand out.

The first one is passion. In order to be a master in anything, you've got to really practice and focus and you have to love what you're doing. Reflective practice is the key to mastery.

The second is adaptive capacity, which I wrote about in *Geeks and Geezers*. Adaptive capacity includes learning. It includes resilience. It includes being a first-class noticer. They are all important.

A third one would be respect, being respectful. In this global age, being respectful to people who are different is not just being tolerant.

Liu: And also different from being humble.

Bennis: It's related, I think, because being humble to me means not knowing everything. Being humble is part of adaptive capacity because if you think you are the smartest guy in the room, you are doomed. Respect is deep, which also means to listen and to really learn from whomever you're with.

I think the fourth thing would be—Bill George emphasizes this in his book—having a sense of knowing who you are. Knowing your values, character, and your authentic being is important.

But I think we need to distinguish further between role authenticity and personal authenticity. I will do things in a role that I find difficult, such as making a decision which will inflict pain. If I feel that the role is requiring things of me which are not congruent with who I am, I cannot stay on that. The choice is: Am I going to surrender my soul and continue working with the organization? Or will I be who I am and resign?

The fifth thing would be courage. I think somehow in this world, you never have the full truth about contexts, about your own biases, about what's going to happen in the next five years. But in moments where you have 70 percent confidence in your intuition and 70 percent knowledge of the situation, you have to act.

So those are five areas. I am sure next year I will think of something else.

Generous Leaders

Liu: People give names to their favorite leadership types—Bill George names "authentic leaders," Jim Collins names "Level 5 Leaders," and Robert Greenleaf names "Servant Leaders." Do you have your favorite name for your favorite leadership type?

Bennis: That's an interesting question. Just to be a little bit different, I would say that I think generosity is a distinct mark of my work. I make a great deal of acknowledgment and of appreciation, which I think is missing in most organizations. I like acknowledgment.

You know, there's a guy who comes to our condo every few months to "detail the car." He refreshes it, he polishes it, he cleans out the interior. It takes two or three hours to do a car. After the first two occasions, I was getting in the car one day, going off to USC to teach, and I said, "Thank you. Looks good." And he said, "Doc, have you *really* looked at your car? Take a look at it." Then I did. I looked at his work. I realized I was being quite perfunctory.

One morning, I was on campus walking along with one of my PhD students. I saw these landscapers. They were making the campus look beautiful, but unnoted, unacknowledged. They got there at six in the morning, and had been on their knees for at least two hours. I said to them: "Thank you for making this campus beautiful, making me feel good when I come here." I didn't think about it. Then on my last birthday, my former student, who is now teaching leadership at a university, emailed me: "I never forget that morning. I will never forget the way you acknowledged the landscapers."

Good leaders genuinely show appreciation, acknowledgment, and respect. In order to become a leader, you also have to have a strong ego and an appropriate amount of ambition, a sense of purpose, and be prepared to be involved in the toughest decisions that may result in people being laid off. How can you be the generous leader and yet make some of these decisions?

Liu: So you are using the term "generous leaders?"

Bennis: Yes, but I don't know whether I'll continue to use it.

Schultz: Showing Respect

Liu: Howard Schultz, the chairman of Starbucks, said he received some advice from you. What advice did you give him? I am curious.

Bennis: I met Howard at a conference years ago and we got to be friends. He's a nice, easy guy. I'll tell you one example, from probably 10 years ago. I was in my office when he called me and said, "Warren, I've got a question for you. Do you have a few minutes?"

I said, "Actually only a few. I have a class in five minutes." So this phone call lasted no more than five minutes.

"So I'm facing a problem I've never faced before," Howard said. "I want to make a major decision, but my direct reports are uniformly against it. I don't know what to do."

So I said: "Well, Howard, has your intuition, your gut instinct, been pretty good in the past?"

When he said yes, I continued: "Well, what you might do is to take your staff immediately off-site, away from your regular company offices, and give them enough opportunity to challenge you, to vent, to tell you about their qualms and reservations. Take two or three hours. You may change your mind. And they might. You may not come to an agreement, but it is important they know they'll be listened to."

That's the conversation. I never followed up what happened until about five years ago, when he came to USC to receive an award. I asked him what the decision was that he'd been worried about. He said, "Whether or not we should open a Starbucks operation in Japan. And all the advice was against it. We paid a consulting firm US$5 million. They said, 'No. Japanese drink tea. They don't like holding a cup of latte, certainly not in public.'" He decided to go ahead anyway.[3]

Liu: So basically your advice is: "You should really listen to your people. Show them that you care about their opinion."

Bennis: Yes. That's an example of respect. Also, guess what? You could change your mind. But ultimately, as the leader, you have to make that big decision.

Sculley: Adaptive Capacity in Action

Liu: I want to ask you about another manager, John Sculley, the former CEO of Apple. In your books, you cited him as an example of a great leader. Do you still think so? Because most people think he was a failure.

Bennis: That is a good question. I think he is a great leader in the right circumstances. When Steve Jobs persuaded him to leave Pepsi where he was destined to be the top guy, he got seduced by Steve Jobs. It's an area that was so different from Pepsi, so I think the circumstances were not congenial to success. He is doing brilliantly now as a venture capitalist. So I think he has adapted very well.

Having failed so publicly and coming back, and being successful, is an example of adaptive capacity, so I wouldn't change my mind. Was John good for Apple? It wasn't a good choice for him.

In this world, you will have downturns or moments where you are no longer a hero for a while. If you learn from such things, this is adaptive capacity.

An Example of Learning

Liu: Do you think your tenure as a university president was a failure or not?

Bennis: [Laughs] I didn't realize you were going to ask all these personal questions. Who do you think you are? Warren Bennis?

Liu: You are not only a leadership guru, but also a leader. You are said to be one of the few leadership gurus that have real experience in leading a large organization.

Bennis: Although I sometimes portray myself as a failure in the stories I tell, looking back, I don't think of myself as a failure for several reasons.

One is that I don't think I could write the stuff I am doing now without having had that experience. I don't feel uneasy. I feel confident when I talk about leadership. I can talk with authority, not just because I have been an author but also because I had 11 years of leading at two universities, very complex organizations. So I feel I am not just talking from my neck up, but also from my experience. That gave me confidence.

What I accomplished was important. We would have gone broke at the University of Cincinnati had I not led a drive, supported by a great team, to become a fully-supported state university. Finally I *learned* so much. How could you learn so much and call it a failure? I can't anyway.

And they finally took 30 years to recognize that. I just got an honorary degree. It's pretty late in coming [laughs]. Now even my former colleagues and board at Cincinnati think I've finally become a success.

Leaders vs. Followers

Liu: You once said that your book *Leaders* should be called *Followers*, and *On Becoming a Leader* should be . . .

Bennis: . . . *On Becoming a Follower.*

Liu: So leaders and followers are two sides of the same coin?

Bennis: I co-authored a book with David Heenan called *Co-Leaders.*

Liu: It's about being second-in-command.

Bennis: Yes. We first wanted to call it *Second Banana*, and the publisher said, "Are you kidding!" He said to me, "What would you think if we changed *On Becoming a Leader* to '*On Becoming a Follower?*' Do you think it would sell any copies in America?"

"Followership" has been a largely neglected field, but not anymore. I wrote some stuff on "followership" a long time ago.

But I am not sure they are the opposite sides of the same coin. In general, what makes a good follower is not always what makes a good leader. The roles are quite different. In that perspective, it is not the opposite side of the same coin. To be an able follower means really to speak truth to power. It means to realize what the mission is.

Drucker or Bennis: Who Said It?

Liu: When I talked to Ronald Heifetz about the difference between leadership and management, he said, "I don't know who originated this but, 'leaders do the right thing and managers do things right.'" I said I thought you had said this.

Bennis: Peter Drucker and I have both been known to have said that. I get a lot of letters asking me who originated it. I may have said it first; I don't know and I don't care. I don't care who gets the credit for it. And given the fact that Peter is older, give it to Peter.

Why "Leading"?

Liu: This question is related to the difference between leadership and management. A middle manager in an organization may ask, "Why do I have to be a leader? Can I just be a manager?" How would you answer that?

Bennis: He must figure out what he wants. That is hard.

I teach a course called "The Art and Adventure of Leadership." It is very hard to gain admission to this class. We take 40 students out of about 300 applicants. I teach with the president of my university, which makes it a big deal.

What I told my students in the last class this semester was, "Leadership is not simply like a marketing course. This is a course about life. This is a course about what you want. This is about what your purposes are, what will give you the most happiness, impact, and benefit. Whom do you want to benefit? What kind of impact do you want? And what will make you happy and lead a good life? You're going to answer those questions. That is what this course is really about."

So the real question for a middle manager is: How much money are you going to need? How much impact do you want to make? Who do you want to benefit? What about your subjective wellbeing? Then they'll get a little closer to how they want to live their lives in leadership situations. And maybe they will get closer to answering that question: Do I want to be a leader?

Endnotes

1 *The Essential Bennis* was published in August 2009, more than a year after the conversation, and includes more than 20 of Bennis's favorite essays, with comments from a number of colleagues and friends on different essays.
2 Bennis told the author in September 2009 that "Project X" has finally morphed into a memoir which will be published with the title *Still Surprised: A Memoir of a Life in Leadership.*
3 Starbucks entered Japan in 1996.

Bill George:
Authentic Leadership

Bill George is Professor of Management Practice at Harvard Business School, where he has taught leadership since 2004. He is the author of four leadership books: *7 Lessons for Leading in Crisis* (2009), *Finding Your Truth North: A Personal Guide* (co-author, 2008), *True North: Discover Your Authentic Leadership* (co-author, 2007), and *Authentic Leadership: Rediscovering the Secrets to Creating Lasting Value* (2003). He started his writing and teaching career after he retired from leading medical-technology company Medtronic, where he was CEO from 1991 to 2001, and chairman from 1996 to 2002.

A number of executives, after retiring from the business stage, have turned to writing or teaching. Few have done so as successfully as Bill George.

George was one of the most successful business leaders in the United States. He joined Medtronic as president and COO in 1989, becoming CEO in 1991 and chairman in 1996. Under his leadership, Medtronic's market capitalization grew from US$1.1 billion to US$60 billion, averaging 35 percent growth per year, a fact of which he is rather proud—even though he has been bashing the idea that the purpose of a corporation is to maximize shareholder value. He was named one of the "Top 25 Business Leaders of the Past 25 Years" by PBS, "Executive of the Year 2001" by the Academy of Management, and "Director of the Year 2001–02" by the National Association of Corporate Directors.

When he retired from Medtronic, companies such as Enron and Arthur Andersen had scandalized and enraged American society and the world, and people like Jeff Skilling and Bernie Ebbers were seen as the epitome of corporate leadership. Intel's Andy Grove (one of the few others to have made successful double careers in practicing business and preaching it) said he was ashamed to be a businessman. No doubt, so was Bill George.

Yet he was inspired too. He wrote the book *Authentic Leadership*, in which he thanked Enron and Arthur Andersen because "we needed this kind of shock therapy to realize that something is sorely missing in many of our corporations." Then what is missing? In one word, leadership; and in two words, authentic leadership, which George advocates as a combination of being who you are and character-based, values-driven leadership.

Neither the title of the book nor its contents were novel or fancy. However, the book caught on, not only because it was—and still is—timely, but also thanks to its author's almost unparalleled credibility. His experience in Medtronic had attested to the fact that a company could do well by doing good; his personal experience of becoming an authentic leader was vividly convincing.

In January 2008, George spoke to me about authentic leadership by phone from his home in Minnesota.

Leading and Teaching

Liu: Your experience is very interesting. You were a very successful CEO, and you are now a management professor. That is very rare. How did this happen?

George: When I became CEO of Medtronic in 1991, I told the board of directors that I should not serve more than 10 years. When I had completed that time in 2001, I was in my late 50s and decided that I wanted to try teaching.

So I went to Switzerland for a working sabbatical at the International Institute for Management Development (IMD) in Lausanne, and at the Swiss Federal Institute of Technology, where I had a joint appointment. I found that I really liked teaching. Then the dean of Harvard Business School, my alma mater—I graduated in 1966—asked me to join the faculty as a professor of management practice and teach the creative new course, "Leadership and Corporate Accountability."

Liu: Are you passionate about teaching?

George: Yes, I like teaching very much. I especially enjoy working with future leaders as well as executives, including the rising generation of Chinese leaders. We have an executive program for Chinese executives taught in Mandarin. They do two weeks in Shanghai, two weeks in Hong Kong, and two weeks at Harvard. I taught four classes on leadership for that course the past three years.

Liu: Were you passionate about teaching when you were a CEO?

George: Yes. Leadership and teaching are closely related, because as CEO you are always coaching people you work with. You try to help them become better leaders. Leading a large global corporation, like I did—Medtronic now has 38,000 employees—involves developing many, many leaders. There must be hundreds of leaders throughout the company for it to be successful. That requires that you are always coaching and helping people develop. It is less about you being a leader than developing other people to lead.

Where Leadership Starts

Liu: You said that a leader's job is not about acquiring a following, but leadership starts with gaining alignment with the mission and values of the organization.

George: In the old days, we used to think in terms of leaders and followers, and that the leader's job was to develop many followers. I think today it is not about leaders and followers: it is about aligning people, or bringing them together around a common mission and a common set of values. That is the most challenging thing; and then empowering other people to step up and lead.

If you have a large global organization, and your organization is in Europe, China, Australia, and Africa, you have to have strong leaders in each of those areas. They have to be able to lead without supervision. But the only way they can do that is if they know the mission and values of the organization; you have to ensure that the values are the same in China, or in Japan, or in the United States. You cannot have different values today.

Liu: But how does a leader find the mission and the values of the organization? Does the leader define and identify these himself and hand them over to the staff?

George: There are two ways. In Medtronic's case, the mission was defined by the founder in 1962, when the company was virtually bankrupt. The mission was defined quite broadly: "To restore people to full life and health." Then the values of treating people with respect and dignity, the quality of each product, and the focus on the patients became part of the company, and they enriched the mission.

For a company that does not have a clear or relevant mission, I think the leader can bring key people together to define a new mission for the company.

Liu: Do these key people include only the top management, or all employees?

George: In the case of IBM, Sam Palmisano, the CEO and a friend of mine, did a very creative thing. Because IBM has 350,000 employees all around the globe, he did an online program called Values Jam.[1] People had an opportunity to log in and for 48 hours—two solid days—give their input on what they thought IBM's values should be.

From that, IBM settled on key values and has been taking these around the world to create what Palmisano calls an Integrated Global Network organization. People in all parts of the world are integrated around a common set of values. That was a very creative way of getting all the employees involved in identifying the company's values and making them feel that they had some ownership of these values.

Leadership is Defined by Life Story

Liu: You said in your book *True North* that an individual's leadership is defined by his or her life story. "Life story" sounds a little bit abstract. Could you elaborate?

George: For 50 years, academics have been trying to define leadership in terms of someone's traits or characteristics: they are aggressive; they are humble; they are intelligent; they are courageous . . . They have been unsuccessful in doing that, because each leader is very different.

We talked to 125 outstanding leaders around the world ranging in age from 23 to 93. We found that what defined all these leaders, regardless of age, was the impact of their individual lives on what was ahead of them. This has then defined what kind of leader they want to become, and where they found their passion to lead and make a difference around the world. It does sound a little abstract, but the important fact is that it defines people, and this becomes much more important than any set of traits or characteristics.

I remember my first trip to China in 1984, meeting with a group of Chinese physicians in Shanghai. These were very brilliant men, who were defined very much by the Cultural Revolution, because they had had to work in the rice fields and give up medicine for a long time. It gave them great passion for their work. They wanted to see a different China in the future. That is just one small example of what I mean.

I know people from countries like Chile or Colombia where they had a great deal of difficulty. They want to go back and use their leadership to improve their home country. In the same way, African-Americans want to improve the lives of African-Americans. Some people are fascinated with technology because early in their lives, like the founder of Medtronic, they got involved in technology and this has defined very much what they want to do in their lives.

Liu: So can we say that "true north" is your passion, your value system?

George: Your True North is what you believe at the deepest level, what defines you—your beliefs, your values, your passions, and the principles you live by. Most people know what their True North is. The problem is that they are pulled off track, caught up in external rewards like money, power, and glory. These things start to define them more than they really believe. Many leaders have lost their way and gone off track because they lost sight of their passions, or they bowed to the pressures of leadership and deviated from their values.

Life Story: Crucible Plus Epiphany

Liu: Not everybody can recognize their true north early in life. So is leadership a journey of exploration?

George: Many people go through a crucible, a very difficult time of their life that becomes a defining moment. My students at Harvard write about their crucibles; almost without exception, they have had significant crucibles that have shaped their lives and their leadership.

Liu: Warren Bennis also talks about how crucibles define leadership.

George: Warren Bennis is a close friend and mentor to me. He wrote the preface to *True North*. He had talked about crucibles in *Geeks and Geezers* and he told me that he had not met anyone who has not experienced a crucible.

Liu: You also used the word "epiphany." What does it mean in relation to "crucible?"

George: You can think about epiphany as a realization. There was a woman in my class who was from one of the Balkan countries. She lived in a very small house that was occupied by enemy soldiers. The rape of her aunt was a traumatic crucible for her. Later, she came to the United States to be educated, and eventually found her way to Harvard. She had an epiphany in understanding the impact of the experience on what she wanted to do in her life, how she wanted it to be different from the life she had grown up with, and eventually how she wanted to go back to her country and help restore it to peace.

Liu: So crucible is an experience, and epiphany is a realization.

George: Exactly. The epiphany may come years later. For example, we interviewed Oprah Winfrey, the famous TV talk show hostess. She had been raped as a young girl by older members of her family, and she thought for many, many years that she was a bad girl. When she was 36 years old, she had an epiphany on the set of her television show when her guest was telling a story very similar to her own and she realized she was not the only one who had had that experience.

From that point on, she changed the message of her show from being about celebrities to empowering people to take responsibility for their lives. From this epiphany about her own life and her own life story, her career has gone straight up. She has been extraordinarily successful in part because she had the epiphany and realized the purpose of her work.

Liu: So can we say, in a simplistic way, that life story is crucible plus epiphany?

George: Yes. There may be other aspects of your life story, all of which form you. Through this epiphany you realize the purpose of your leadership, and you realize leadership is not about you or your success. It's about your ability to build a team that can make a positive difference.

Say, for example, you start a new company in China with a view to making a lot of money for yourself. Later, though, you come to realize that there's more to it than this: you want to build a company that helps China by creating jobs for others. This is a very different approach. One is all about you: the other is about trying to help others. That is where the epiphany comes in.

Liu: So for those people who have not become a leader, or who have failed as a leader, does that mean that they have not had their epiphany?

George: That failure may be their crucible that forces them to look at who they are. They may get caught up in how much money they make, how much publicity they get, and how much success they have in the eyes of the world, rather than fulfilling something that is more important at a deeper level.

All Great Leaders are Authentic

Liu: You said just now that you don't agree that great leaders share some common traits or characteristics.

George: Right. I do not agree. Great leaders are very, very different individuals. Some leaders are very aggressive, and some leaders are very humble. Some leaders are brilliant, and some leaders have only average intelligence. For example, A. G. Lafley, CEO of Procter & Gamble,[2] is an outstanding leader, who is wise and humble, in spite of his enormous success.

Liu: You also once said that authentic leadership is something like Jim Collins' Level 5 Leadership.

George: Yes, they're quite similar. The key thing is being your authentic self, not trying to emulate, not trying to be like someone else, not trying to emulate Jack Welch.

Liu: But Jim Collins once said that he thinks great leaders share one common characteristic, which is willful humility. Level 5 Leaders are, by his definition, humble. They are willfully humble.

George: I don't think all great leaders are humble. There are many great leaders who are humble, but many are not. For example, Bill Gates has done great things in Microsoft, but he is not humble.

Liu: So authenticity, which you advocate, is not a common characteristic.

George: I wouldn't call authenticity a characteristic. Some people are authentically humble, and some are authentically ambitious. Or some people are dynamic and aggressive, and some people are shy. All of them can be great leaders if they stay true to their authentic character. Authenticity is not a characteristic; it is who you are. It means knowing who you are and what your purpose is.

Liu: That may be disappointing to many people. They go to business schools, leadership development workshops, or seminars to learn how to become a leader. And you are telling them that there is no universal recipe.

George: That's correct. A lot of people are looking for a quick fix. They want a few quick traits they can emulate to become a leader, and they always fail. They never become successful leaders because they are not being themselves.

There is no quick fix. It is hard work. You have to spend a lifetime developing yourself as a leader. It never stops. I am still trying to develop myself as a leader.

Liu: So you are not saying that authentic leadership is an option of leadership. What you are saying is that great leadership is authentic leadership.

George: Exactly. It is fundamental to leadership. People like Larry Ellison at Oracle and Carly Fiorina at HP may get a lot of newspaper publicity, but they are not authentic leaders.

Setting a Bad Example

Liu: Let's talk about Bob Nardelli. You named him as an example of poor leadership.

George: Bob Nardelli is a very good manager. He knows how to manage a budget, how to cut costs, but he could not create a great business. It's more about Bob Nardelli and how much money he gets. But I would not consider him an authentic leader. That may be one reason he was not chosen to be CEO at General Electric. It may be the reason he failed at Home Depot, and could not succeed at Chrysler.[3] He may be successful at cutting costs—anyone can cut costs—but building a great enterprise is very hard.

General Electric CEO Jeff Immelt is a very authentic leader who will be very successful at GE in the long run.

Liu: You said Nardelli is a great manager. What is the difference between leadership and management?

George: Managers can manage budgets, numbers, and systems, all the things you learn at business school, but may not inspire and empower other people to lead, and may not create a great enterprise. When he went to Home Depot, Nardelli fired 70 out of 71 vice presidents. In the end no one knew the retail business, and he failed to create a great business.

Liu: Some people might say that Nardelli is one type of leader and some companies need this kind of leader.

George: Only in the short term. They may need a Bob Nardelli to come in and do a financial turnaround. But this does not require a great leader. A great leader would be someone like Howard Schultz of Starbucks, who created a great enterprise all around the world, and then was himself replaced with a manager named Jim Donald. Starbucks started going downhill, so Schultz returned to Starbucks to get the company back on track because they were losing sight of their unique character.

Liu: I wrote an essay about Starbucks in China. They expanded very quickly. But they didn't do very well in customer service.

George: Maybe too quickly, and perhaps they didn't understand the needs of Chinese customers.

Setting a Great Example

Liu: You think Andrea Jung is a very good example of authentic leadership, I believe.

George: One of the very best. She is, you may know, of Chinese-Canadian origin. Her father was a professor from Shanghai. Her mother was a doctor from Hong Kong. They married, moved to Toronto, and eventually came to the United States when he became a professor at MIT in Boston.

Andrea Jung has the largest organization in the world: six million people work with Avon Products. She was originally passed over for CEO and almost quit. One of the company's board members told her that she should follow her compass, not her clock. When she became CEO, she changed the mission of Avon Products from cosmetics to the empowerment of women.

She did this because she realized that what makes Avon is helping women who are poor achieve economic self-sufficiency. The women borrow the money to buy inventory, and then build the business to be successful. So it is kind of like microenterprise, or microfinance.

She is one of the most successful leaders in the world, and was named one of the American Best Leaders in 2007. Andrea is a very authentic and humble person who has never forgotten her Chinese roots. She was raised in a family where discipline and commitment were very important. If she makes a commitment, she will always be true to it.

Liu: I told her story in one of the workshops I hosted for Chinese business managers, which was about self-leadership. Actually the story is from you, where she said that she didn't feel passionate about making luxury goods for the upper class.

George: You understand very well. At that time, she was in line to become CEO at Niemen Marcus, a very upscale department store. She was its executive vice president at just 31. At 35, she quit because she didn't want to spend the rest of her life making luxury goods for upper-class women. She wanted to do something for a full range of people. That is why she is so passionate about Avon. "If people can't see the passion I have for this company," she said, "then I can't be their leader."

Serving the Customer First

Liu: Going back to Bob Nardelli: the Chrysler board still selected him after he failed at Home Depot. So perhaps your idea about authentic leadership is not commonly shared in the United States. It seems that shareholders think that people like Nardelli can create shareholder value.

George: In the long run you have to create both stakeholder value and stockholder value. But Nardelli was chosen to head Chrysler because they wanted a cost-cutter. They wanted somebody to go in and reduce costs, and then the owners would sell the company in three years. They did not want to create great automobiles. Eventually, Chrysler went bankrupt when the market turned down, and even today is continuing to lose market share.

Liu: Then let's talk about the purpose of a company. What is a company for?

George: The purpose of a company starts with providing unique value to its customers. It doesn't start with serving the shareholders. Any company that doesn't create greater value for their customers than their competitors do will be eventually out of business. So it is critical for a company to create value for its customers, and then that's how you create value for your shareholders.

Liu: Shareholders are mostly "short-termists." They are not farsighted.

George: This is a very big problem in the US, where many shareholders are looking to make quick money. In the end, they probably won't do as well. Shareholders who invest in a company for a long time, like Warren Buffett, are the most successful in the long-term.

Other people who just want to make money by buying and selling stocks never create great companies.

Liu: But that makes the job of the leader, of the CEO, very difficult.

George: Very difficult, particularly in a place like the United States, where there is such a short-term orientation. In China, people have a much longer orientation. This is why Chinese companies are becoming so competitive, because they have a longer point of view.

Liu: When you were a CEO, did you have conflicts with the board regarding long-term strategy?

George: No. The board of Medtronic was very anxious to build a company for the long term. The stock value went from US$1.1 billion to US$60 billion because we had a long-term orientation.

Liu: You were lucky to have that board. For CEOs who are not so lucky, what is your advice?

George: You have to educate the board and get the board committed to the long term. For instance, I am on the board of Exxon Mobil, the world's largest company, with a US$400 billion market capitalization. It has a very long-term orientation. All the compensation for the executives is based upon long-term performance, not short-term performance.

Liu: The CEO of a Chinese company listed on the New York Stock Exchange actually said to me that he regretted being listed on Wall Street. He wants to focus on value he creates for customers, but Wall Street pushes him to focus on numbers.

George: If you have a long-term view, sometimes you need the courage to stand up to Wall Street, rather than do what the security analysts tell you to do. A lot of people are not that courageous and they wind up destroying great companies. Bristol–Meyers, for example, was once a great pharmaceutical company. Now it is struggling because its management was so short-term oriented.

I am on the board of a Swiss company called Novartis, one of the greatest pharmaceutical companies in the world. Dan Vasella, the CEO, whom I have written about in *True North,* has a very long-term orientation. It takes 12 years to develop new drugs. If you try to do it in less time, you will fail. Unless you have a long-term orientation, you cannot create a great drug company, period. It is not possible.

Business Ethics in China

Liu: You have taught Chinese executives. What have you found in them that is special?

George: On the positive side, Chinese executives tend to be very down-to-earth, very practical people. They are very good business people, and have a very long-term view. This applies not only to people from mainland China, but also Chinese business people who live in Hong Kong, Singapore, or Vancouver.

The biggest concern I have about China is that even though your country has Confucian principles, there are no clear business ethics today.

We had a great debate on business ethics among the Chinese I taught at the class at Harvard. One businessman said he had decided to be totally ethical. He had thought he would lose 30 percent of business, but it had actually increased 10 percent. Other people in the class said it was not possible and you had to pay bribes. There was a huge debate, which I just listened to. Since the modern capitalist system is new in China, it is still developing its ethical standards.

One of the things we talked about with the Chinese executives was Siemens, a German company that had admitted to paying US$2 billion in bribes. Several Chinese executives in the room said that they had to compete with Siemens. Siemens and General Electric used to be equivalent companies. But GE has always been very ethical. It has made mistakes, but it has been very ethical. Now Siemens has been hurt by the ethics scandal, but under new leadership, it is going forward.

Liu: Sometimes when I talk to Chinese executives, using American or European examples, they say, "We're different. There are so many opportunities here in China. Everything is so fast."

George: This is why your work is so important in China. I think Chinese executives today are eager to think about how they operate within the context of a communist government and a capitalistic system, which is a new model. As I have written in my blog, my personal belief is that capitalism is more important than democracy at this stage of development.

China is developing a strong capitalistic system that can give people economic self-sufficiency and give people freedom. Eventually it will develop into a more democratic country. In Iraq, we have imposed democracy, but there is no economy there. There is no capitalism, no free-enterprise system. I think the Chinese system is a very good model for developing countries.

Endnotes

1 According to IBM's website, Values Jam lasted for 72 hours and IBM had 319,000 employees then.
2 A. G. Lafley has since retired from P&G.
3 Chrysler filed for bankruptcy on April 30, 2009 and was out of bankruptcy on June 10, 2009 when Bob Nardelli stepped down as CEO.

PART II

Leadership in Organizations

Peter Senge: Leading a Learning Organization

Peter Senge is a Senior Lecturer at the Massachusetts Institute of Technology and Founding Chair of the Society for Organizational Learning (SOL), a global community of corporations, researchers, and consultants dedicated to the "interdependent development of people and their institutions." Author of the widely acclaimed book *The Fifth Discipline: The Art and Practice of the Learning Organization* (1990, revised in 2006), Senge is seen as the spokesperson of the Learning Organization movement and recognized as one of most influential management gurus in the world. He has also co-authored the following books: *The Fifth Discipline Field Book* (1994), *The Dance of Change* (1999), *Schools That Learn* (2000), *Presence* (2004), and *The Necessary Revolution* (2008).

While the corporate world generally sees only one side of Peter Senge—management guru, bestselling author and advocate of the Learning Organization—there is another: a cultivator who practices meditation on a daily basis, an explorer of human wisdom and spirit, an individual who spends his whole life in "becoming a human being."

Senge's two sides are actually an integrated whole. As he said to Nan Huaijin,[1] a master of Chinese traditional cultures, the purpose of his cultivation is to make a contribution to humankind. When he started out as a doctoral student, he had no interest in business at all. However, with a sense of purpose, he found his own way of making a contribution: being the advocate of the five disciplines—personal mastery, mental models, shared vision, team learning, and systems thinking—of a learning organization.

Senge is typically viewed as a guru in the field of organizational learning, not leadership. However, the two areas overlap. As he pointed out in the first edition of *The Fifth Discipline*, the five disciplines of a learning organization can also be called the disciplines of leadership; people who have mastered them will be the natural leaders of learning organizations.

I spoke with Senge about leadership—in person, over the phone, and by email—on various occasions in 2008 and 2009. The following dialog is an approved edited version of our exchanges of ideas.

Rediscovering Leadership

Liu: In your foreword to my Chinese book *Master Classes of Leadership* you wrote that "few words are used more frequently and counterproductively today than 'leadership.'" What does leadership mean to you?

Senge: First, there is profound confusion about what the very word means. Most often, "leader" is used as a synonym for "boss," the person "at the top," those in the most senior positions—as when people say, "the problem in our company is the leaders are afraid of change that threatens their power." While this may very well be an accurate assessment about those in positions of authority, to define those with positional authority as "the leaders" is redundant and disempowering. At the least, it confuses formal authority, as embodied in positions like CEO or president, with leadership. At the worst, it sends the signal that only those in such positions are "the leaders"—and, by definition, no one else.

Interestingly, "leader as boss" also deviates from the root meaning of the English verb "to lead," which comes from an Indo-European root, *leith*, "to step across a threshold." In this sense, leadership is an act of stepping ahead and of doing so in a way that can inspire others—"inspire" is another word long associated with leadership, and which appropriately means "to breathe life into." So, a deeper understanding of leadership as action, as opposed to leadership as position, illuminates capacities that people have always valued: courage, which, by the way, comes from a French word meaning "tears or openings of the heart," taking risk, and bringing to life a challenging undertaking in ways that create a social field of imagination, commitment, and trust among others.

Liu: If we look up the word "threshold" in Webster's, we find three meanings: firstly, the plank, stone, or piece of timber that lies under the door; secondly, end, boundary, or outset; and thirdly, a point or a level above which something will take place. In which sense of the word does leadership relate to?

Senge: The threshold to which *leith* refers, in my understanding, is when one steps ahead across a zone of uncertainty, or fear, or incompetence, or whatever else, associated with doing something that requires real courage. So, it is an image that is more metaphorical than literal, although I personally often picture it like a chasm.

Each of the dictionary definitions is accurate in a way. It is definitely a boundary, as between a territory in which I am comfortable or familiar with and one where I am uncomfortable and unfamiliar. It can also be seen as an entryway where one moves from one space into another, or a portal through which one must pass in order to enter a different space. Interestingly, Otto Scharmer claims that the threshold was also historically associated with *dying*, as in "What must I be willing to let go of in order to enter this new place?" for it is what we hold on to—assumptions, identified images, our sense of competence—that will keep us from crossing this threshold.

Liu: Why is it counterproductive to associate leadership only with people at the top?

Senge: Leadership is a subject about which people have strong views and where the weight of history and established habits of thinking and acting is considerable. It is because of those deeply engrained habits that we tend to obsess about leadership as positional authority. Whether because of personal ambition to gain such positions, or because of fear of how others with such positional power may affect us, or because of romantic hopes that a new "hero leader" will come to save us, the cult of hierarchical leadership is not likely to diminish any time soon.

It is not that effective leadership from people in executive or hierarchical positions is unimportant—nothing could be further from the truth. But obsessing about positional leadership tragically diverts attention in an era where, everywhere we turn, we confront problems where hierarchical leadership alone, no matter how effective, is inadequate.

For example, businesses everywhere seek to become more innovative. But this requires a willingness of leaders throughout an organization to take risks and learn from putting daring new ideas into practice. Successful innovation comes from synergy between learning at many levels that is technical, market-oriented, strategic and operational, and that eventually fosters new thinking and new practices that are widespread and lasting. Such changes cannot be driven only from the top.

Moreover, increasingly the innovation needed most will reshape larger systems that go beyond individual organizations, like value chains, industries, cities and economic regions and, ultimately, society. Not only can this not be accomplished by individual organizations, it cannot be accomplished without cross-sector innovation that will involve business, government and civil society, and levels of cooperation that are unprecedented. Nurturing and aligning the diverse forms of leadership needed for systemic change is the leadership challenge of our age. It is such challenges that make rediscovering a deeper understanding of leadership so important.

Liu: In *The Fifth Discipline*, you said leaders have three roles in an organization: the designer, the servant, and the teacher.

Senge: Yes. I think that is still a useful way to think about executive leadership. In the first edition of the book, I probably just used the word "leader." I think in the revised edition, I used the words "executive leader." That is particularly true when you are in a senior position where you have very important work to do on all three of these levels.

I think it is also true of all types of leaders. You must know how you help other people, your commitment to purpose, and your ability to think about not just the problems, but also the sources of problems and how they arise from the organizational design.

Learning vs. Teaching

Liu: Probably you have heard the term "Teaching Organization," as used by Professor Noel Tichy. He said that the emphasis on the learning organization is limiting because everybody should not only learn, but also teach. Would you like to comment on this?

Senge: I don't disagree. I think he is using the word "learn" in a slightly different way though. One of the problems with the word "learning" is that people often think of it in terms of a schoolroom.

I always think learning is more like what happens to any group— a team, a theater troupe, a group of musicians—that is, enhancing its capacity to create the results it really wants.

The schoolroom is more about a method, not the nature of learning itself. Learning, to me, is more fundamental and teaching is more a method. Learning is a process whereby we grow and develop as human beings.

Oftentimes the most powerful way of learning is to teach, right? First off, you want to help other people. So that's the impulse to teach. But secondly, the process of helping others is to learn: deepening your own learning.

So I think learning is more fundamental than teaching. Teaching is an activity we do. Learning is really at the core of all types of development, whether it is meditative cultivation, or learning to be a physicist, or to play the violin. To me, learning is at the heart of humanness.

Liu: I think Professor Tichy was talking about it in the context of an organization. He gave an example like this: if one person learns something but holds it to himself, if he does not teach others, it is not good for the organization.

Senge: I agree completely. But notice, again, he is using the word "learn" as the individual phenomenon. As I said, again, the key learning in any organization is always collective. Lots of people forget that, because they go back to thinking about the school when they think about learning.

So I agree with what he said, of course. I said something very much like that in the first edition of *The Fifth Discipline*: Individual learning ultimately is irrelevant because very little value is created in any organization by individuals by themselves.

Leading a Learning Town?

Liu: A friend of mine is the mayor of a small town in China. But, as you know, by American standards, it is not small at all. He said to me, "I am advocating turning my town into a learning town." That amazed me. Do you think it is possible to turn a whole town into a Learning Organization?

Senge: I think it's a great aspiration. I don't know if it's possible, but it's a really good goal. To me it would have two kinds of meaning.

The first would be that the institutions in the community, in the town—the schools, the governmental institutions, the businesses, and the hospitals—can continually learn to be Learning Organizations. They are continually developing their ability to have visions, to reflect on their mental models, and so on.

Secondly, you would like to think about the community as a whole developing a lot of capabilities. In some sense, I don't think it is so complicated. What does it mean for those people living together? That is to continually ask: What really matters to us?

I will take a simple example to make it less abstract. If I live in the community, one of the most important things for me would be the lives of the children because they are our future. We all have a biological, as well as a social, responsibility to the children. So part of my vision for a community is that of children growing up and becoming healthy human beings. They are learning about humanness. They are embarking on a lifelong journey of health, wellbeing, and contribution because to be a human being is to learn more and more about how to contribute to the world of others.

So one of the things I would always look at first is how healthy the children are. That includes how effective the schools are. But a lot of times, when we look at the schools we just look at test scores. The children are not growing up to be healthy human beings. They don't have a sense of purpose. They don't have a sense of their uniqueness as human beings. They don't necessarily have a desire to contribute to others. There are basic things that all of us around the world would kind of agree on about what is a healthy environment for children to grow up in. And very few of us would say we have it.

Indicators for a Learning Organization

Liu: It sounds like schools are one indicator you use when looking at a community. Do you have such an indicator when looking at a company?

Senge: I would say there's no one indicator. We did some research years ago: Could we create defining indicators for a Learning Organization? I personally have mixed feelings about this.

Whenever we are trying to learn anything, individually or collectively, we need to be able to judge how well we are doing; so you create measures, right? If you are a basketball team, you pay attention to how many games you win and how well you shoot. Any learning requires indicators. So that part I think is fine.

The key is that the learners need to create and use the indicators. A common problem occurs when a manager who loves to have some indicators, gets consultants in to come up with some. Then you have a completely different kind of process when somebody is trying to impose measures on somebody else. I think some of that is inescapable; that is in part of what management does. Management always creates metrics and indicators.

But good managers continually work to make sure these indicators are really meaningful to people, and people have a genuine desire to achieve these things. This is the principle of aspiration in our work, that indicators are only useful if they are aligned with people's aspirations.

It is inherent in any learning process that learners will want to know how well they are doing so they can get better. So indicators are fine. But one set of indicators universally applied will never be meaningful.

People in any organization will be able to really get excited about the question: What is success? What does it mean to us? How can we measure it for our own benefit so we can continually improve? If you really get people to engage themselves, and not just force them, they get very passionate.

Several years ago, a researcher did a case study in China. The workers in an electronics company got very passionate about eliminating waste water, as a sign that they had a good company. They developed a vision of eliminating waste water. The water leaving the plant would be cleaner than the water that came into the plant. They would bottle and drink the water themselves. And they did. They bottled and drank the water that came out of the plant as a sign of their commitment to creating no waste water in their community [laughs].

This small story indicates that if you let people develop indicators that are consistent with what they really care about, they will really watch the indicators. Indicators are very important, but the key is that they have to align with what people really care about.

Indicators are about business performance, about process, about the health and wellbeing of the members of your organization and of the larger community. As a way of contributing to the town, that same company hired a lot of people from the town who had failed to pass the entrance examination to top Chinese universities. It found that these people could be excellent employees and they contributed to the health and wellbeing of the community. I think that says a lot about indicators.

Two Levels of Effective Teaching

Liu: Do you know about the book *Nan Huaijin and Peter Senge*?

Senge: [Laughs] Yes. I've seen a copy, but it is only in Chinese, so I don't know it in detail.

Liu: It is basically the transcription of the continuing dialog you both had from 2003 to 2006. Were you able to meet him after that?

Senge: Yes. In 2007, we did a program at The Great Learning Center he built outside Shanghai. We had a group of people from around the world, called ELIAS[2] Fellows. It was a new leadership development program that involved quite a few different companies and NGOs. One part of it was a two-week learning journey to China, including five days spent at the Center. I continue to visit him once or twice a year.

Liu: Actually that book was a surprise to many people, including me. People know about Master Nan, and they know about you. But they didn't know about the special connection between you two. How important is Master Nan to you?

Senge: Well, all of us need teachers at different times. Different people have been important teachers at different times in my life. Virtually all my life, I have had a deep interest in Chinese culture, and particularly Chinese wisdom traditions. Mostly I pursue this interest by reading and meeting different people.

When I had the chance to meet Master Nan, it was an opportunity for me to really go much deeper. Of course you can only understand these things well if you have to become, to use a common term in China, a "cultivator." You have to become a serious practitioner in meditation or whatever other disciplines you follow.

I have actually been doing this for many years. I was first introduced to Zen, or *Chan* as you would say in Chinese, when I was in college. So I have been a meditator for a very long time. But I have had a chance to deepen my meditation practice considerably since I got to know Master Nan.

When you are around someone like Master Nan, you are around a lot of people who are also very serious about their personal development. I have enjoyed being around people like economists, accountants, business people, and teachers, who like myself are very active in the world. My greatest interest really is not meditation or cultivation in isolation, but how it can help me, and how I, in turn, can be helpful to others in bringing a deeper understanding of humanness to all of our organizations.

Liu: So you are saying you not only learn from Master Nan, but also learn from the people around him.

Senge: Right. This is very similar to the work we have done for a long, long time. In organizations, sometimes people mistake the word "learning" as being just about individual learning. I really think most powerful learning processes are both individual and collective.

It is no coincidence that spiritual communities, for example, have been communities for thousands of years. There is a lot of important learning that really occurs collectively. So, yes, it has been very useful for me to also get to know a lot of Master Nan's students and the community.

Over the years, particularly in the last two or three years, we have started to bring different groups together. So there is a greater intersection now between my study of the Chinese traditions and the relevant use of that understanding in schools and organizations. The ELIAS program is one example.

So, yes, I think there are always two levels of effective teaching. One is what the teacher says and does, and the other is the whole larger climate or environment a great teacher will create.

Becoming a Human Being

Liu: Frankly, I don't understand most of content of *Nan Huaijin and Peter Senge*. Could you explain something of what you have learned from Master Nan or people around him?

Senge: Sure. I am not surprised you have some difficulty with it. Although I am not able to read the book itself, I remember a lot of the conversations. For most of the time, they were fairly esoteric, exploring complex subjects in the Buddhist, Taoist, or Confucian traditions. The book is not necessarily very easy for someone who is not really familiar with a lot of this. Keep in mind, I have been studying this for many years and very often I will take one particular book and spend maybe a year or two studying it.

To answer your question, I would say the experience for me has been the extension of many things I have studied throughout my life.

I made a comment earlier that I believe much of the work we have been doing for more than two decades—really almost three decades—has been how to bring a deeper understanding of humanness into businesses, into schools, into all kinds of organizations.

In modern society, I think we really have a limited understanding of what it means to be a human being. People typically think you are born a human being. But in all sorts of cultivation traditions, not just Buddhism or Taoism, but in virtually all cultivation traditions, whether Eastern or Western, the basic idea is that you spend your life becoming a human being. You are not born a human being.

This is a very important idea, but it makes very little sense to modern people because they pay very little attention to the way their mind works, to the connections between their mind and their body, to the source of their wellbeing. We think happiness depends upon what we buy, although we all know at some level that this is not true. This is the fundamental deceit of modern consumer culture.

The American philosopher Eric Hoffer once said, "You can never get enough of what you don't need to make you happy." So you always want more and more. This is the basic problem not only for us personally, but also for the world as a whole.

At some level, we have to understand better what really matters to us. In *The Fifth Discipline* you see one of the cornerstones of our work is Personal Mastery, one of the five disciplines. One key to Personal Mastery is Personal Vision. In your life, you must continually ask the question: What really matters to me? What is really important? It is not about getting the final answer. The point is that it becomes a very active question.

Sitting behind our work is the belief that you spend your life continually asking what really matters, and orienting your life around things that really matter to you. It seems very simple, but in fact most people don't do it because they don't have a deep enough understanding of how to approach the domains of personal vision.

That is one example. There are many, many examples, all of which will directly relate to our work. Another example would be the area of Mental Models that has always been very central to our work.

What is a mental model? It is an internal construction of reality. We all live in this way. We have mental models of our family, of our companies, and of our societies. We have mental models of everything we interact with because as human beings we interact through our consciousness.

The more we can understand how these mental models come about, the more we can learn in any organizational setting. The key challenge every organization faces is how people's mental models become rigid. This is what causes companies to go out of business— because they have rigid pictures of realities. They can't let go.

One of the key ideas in many meditative practices is "let it go." You notice the content of your thoughts, and then, let it go. That is a fundamental practice for working with mental models. Not that you have to destroy your mental model, but you have to release it. You can't hold on to it.

The Purpose of a Business

Liu: There is actually one part in the book I can understand. When somebody brought up the idea of educating entrepreneurs, Master Nan commented that there were no real entrepreneurs in China because they didn't understand the meaning of "enterprise." In Chinese, he said, "enterprise" means "meaningful mission with enduring value" but, now, everybody was just making money and didn't understand what an enterprise was.

You just said not every human being understands what being a human being is. I think we can apply it to the corporate level, right?

Senge: Right.

Liu: Could you say something about why we gather a group of people to form an enterprise? What is the purpose of a company?

Senge: These are very, very important questions. I think they are among the most important questions in our discussion today. Part of our work for a long time has been to distinguish between two different ways of thinking about business: one old, one new.

The newer one is from business schools. If you take a business strategy course, or if you look at the approach to consulting that most strategic-management consulting firms take, they usually start off with the first principle that says something like: The purpose of the business is to maximize the return on invested capital. And that is called the modern "financial theorem of the firm."

I personally think it is a tremendous distortion of what it takes to build a really good business because business is really a human community. It's a living system. There is a good book on this, the author of which—Arie de Geus, a retired executive from Shell—has been a very important teacher to me.

Liu: I read the book, *The Living Company*. I remember you wrote the foreword to it, in which you talked about the meaning of "business" (*Sheng Yi*) in Chinese, which is "life and meaning."

Senge: So you know exactly what I am talking about. I think it is an important idea that a company is a human community first. Peter Drucker is very eloquent about this. He used to say, "Profit for a company is like oxygen for a person." You have to have the oxygen, but that's not your purpose. That's a necessary condition.

We had a big meeting in Boston just a couple of months ago to consider the concept of the corporation for the twenty-first century. It involved some real elders from the business community, including Arie de Geus and a variety of legal scholars who know a lot of the history of the legal definitions of corporations.

One of interesting things that was pointed out was that traditionally, even in the West, the idea was that it was a privilege, not a right, to make profit. To organize a business in order to make money, and to distribute the money to the owners of the business, you had to have a charter which had a term. After a certain period, the charter would naturally be made void. You had to be re-chartered. You had to keep proving that your business actually contributed to society.

This is exactly what Master Nan was talking about: the nature of real entrepreneurs. I think this is an idea that people have understood for a long time.

Endnotes

1 Nan Huaijin (born 1918) is widely considered to be one of the few living masters of Chinese traditional cultures.

2 Acronym for Emerging Leadership for Innovation Across the Sectors.

CHAPTER 5

Noel Tichy: Leading a Teaching Organization

Noel Tichy is a Professor of Management & Organizations at the Ross School of Business at the University of Michigan, where he directs the Global Business Partnership. From 1985–87, he was Manager of Management Education for General Electric, where he directed its worldwide development efforts. Among the many books he has co-authored are: *Judgment: How Winning Leaders Make Great Calls* (2007), *The Cycle of Leadership: How Great Leaders Teach Their Companies to Win* (2002), *The Leadership Engine: How Winning Companies Build Leaders at Every Level* (1997), and *Control Your Destiny or Someone Else Will: How Jack Welch is Making General Electric the World's Most Competitive Company* (1993).

Not Harvard. Not Wharton. Not London Business School, or INSEAD in Paris. Arguably, the world's best business school is the fabled Crotonville in Ossining, NY, where General Electric (GE) has located its management-training center since 1956. Now called the John F. Welch Leadership Development Center in honor of its former CEO Jack Welch, under whose leadership it flourished, Crotonville has developed into both a talent machine producing leaders at every corporate level, and a change-driving engine.

After becoming CEO in 1981, Welch reinvented Crotonville and legend has it that he himself taught there every two weeks, missing only one session (when he had heart bypass surgery) during his 20-year tenure as CEO.

Crotonville is much more than a corporate university. It is legendary for producing CEOs for many Fortune 500 companies. Nitin Nohria, a Harvard Business School professor, was reported as saying in 2003 that "There's reason to believe that they are a better training ground than we are."[1]

Noel Tichy was instrumental in Crotonville's development. At Jack Welch's invitation, Tichy left the University of Michigan in 1985 to become head of GE's management training center, and in that capacity he witnessed, participated in, and facilitated the transformation of GE as an insider. He recalls that this was the largest and best leadership laboratory in the world where, during his two-year tenure, he learned more about leadership than he had in the previous 15 years.

Returning to the University of Michigan, he started to teach what he had learned at GE, not only to MBA students and business executives, but also to the army, educational and healthcare institutions, and other not-for-profit organizations.

At a hotel in Shanghai in June 2008, after hosting a one-day leadership development session for a group of global business executives, Noel Tichy sat down with me for a vibrant one-on-one session.

Leadership is Transformational

Liu: How do you define leadership? I have read two definitions in your book. One is "leadership is the ability to see reality as it really is and to mobilize the appropriate response." The other is "leadership is the capacity to get things done through others by changing people's mindsets and energizing them into action."

Tichy: I think I'll start with the second one. The way I often teach is "leadership is accomplishing something through other people that wouldn't have happened without you." It does not require a formal position. It is asking: "Have I made something happen?" The true leader makes things happen through other people that wouldn't happen without him. That is fundamental to being a leader.

To be a good leader, you have to have a teachable point of view; you have to be able to develop other leaders, and so forth.

Liu: A lot of business thinkers differentiate leadership from management. Do you do that?

Tichy: There is a short phrase: "Managers do things the right way, and leaders do the right things." I think a good leader needs managerial skills, but having managerial skills doesn't necessarily make a good leader. So I make that distinction. But fundamentally, I go back to "if you are a leader, you make things happen in the world that wouldn't have happened without you."

Liu: Don't managers also make things happen through other people? That is what we expect managers to do well.

Tichy: James McGregor Burns, in a great book called *Leadership*, differentiated between transactional and transformational leadership. Transactional leadership is really management, and transformational leadership is leadership.

I did a book back in the mid-1980s that was built out of what Burns called *The Transformational Leader*, which was why Jack Welch hired me to run Crotonville. The book had a very simple premise at that time—I think we've reached that time again—that we were (and we will forever be) in need of transformational leaders. A transformational leader is someone who fundamentally transforms the organization, takes it to a different level, and it never goes back.

Transforming an organization is a dramatic act. Through transformation you unleash fear and hope, change and resistance. I often say transformation is a three-act drama. Act I is waking the organization up to meet the change. Act II is giving a vision of where you take it. And the third act is re-architecting the organization, the human resources, and the structure to fit the vision. By the time you finish Act III, the world will have changed and you will need to start all over.

So I built the whole framework around helping people be transformational leaders. I think I'll go back fundamentally to Burns's saying that management is transactional. With leadership, we are talking transformational.

Leadership is Top-Down

Liu: In the preface to *The Leadership Engine*, you stated that "leadership was the key determinant of success, not processes, culture, techniques, or scientific management, but energized visionary leaders who could make things happen." If people say that you might have overemphasized leadership, what is your defense?

Tichy: How could you ever overemphasize leadership? Seriously, say more about what you are getting at—I emphasize leadership at the expense of process, structure, and systems?

Liu: Henry Mintzberg once wrote an article criticizing the myth of the charismatic leader and questioning whether Lou Gerstner alone had been responsible for turning IBM around, as legend had it. He raised the question of the contribution made by other people in IBM. In his view, the turnaround could not be attributed to Gerstner alone.

Tichy: As you know from my work, I believe you have to have leaders at all levels. You have somebody at the top that is the head leader/teacher. Everything he or she does is designed to engage thousands of people in the organization as leaders. But without a leader at the top, this won't happen.

Mintzberg has launched a kind of anti-leadership movement in leadership. Jim Collins also has kind of an anti-leadership view. This really misses the reality. Jack Welch, for example, invested most of his time and energy in developing leaders at all levels. Crotonville was about making everyone of those kids who had just gotten off the campus, those first-time leaders, a leader. It's having many CEOs at every single level. It's what A. G. Lafley does at P&G.[2]

None of that would have happened without someone at the top. That there is someone at the top doesn't mean that he is an autocrat. Gerstner was somebody who mobilized thousands of people.

Liu: In one interview you said "bottom-up is junk."

Tichy: Absolutely. Never saw that happen in my life. It's non-existent. Now the paradox is the top has to engage the bottom and then you can get bottom-up ideas. So, paradoxically, it's top-down to get bottom-up.

The CEO as Head Teacher

Liu: I think most people will agree instinctively that leaders should be learners. You have been saying that leaders should be teachers. You've written several books on this subject. Tell me why.

Tichy: I often jokingly, but in a serious vein, say: Look, learning can be fun and exciting but if it does not turn into teaching and making the organization better it is not useful. The "learning organization" movement in the US held up companies like Digital Equipment as role models. Digital Equipment is dead now because the learning never translated into teaching and action in the marketplace. So learning has to further the organization's performance. The learners must turn their learning into teaching, and that makes everybody better.

Learning is necessary but not sufficient. The teaching I am talking about is not command and control one way, but creating a virtuous teaching cycle.

Liu: People will probably agree that leaders should be teachers, or that teacher should be one of a leader's many roles. But what you actually say is that teaching is the leader's major role. Is that right?

Tichy: The higher the hierarchy goes, the more important it is, because if you are not doing it, you are doing the work. At General Electric, Jeff Immelt is not making jet engines or any other products, but he is really investing in the human capital side of the organization. So he is the head teacher. Every day his job is to help the organization get smarter and more aligned. And it's not one-way teaching.

One of the many fascinating things that Jeff Immelt did was to put billions of dollars in a new R&D investment and create a "Crotonville" at the R&D center in order to get the businesses more aligned and involved in virtuous teaching cycles. All business leaders were required, four times a year, to bring the whole team up there and hang out with the scientists. That to me is an example of setting the stage for leaders to teach and creating virtuous teaching cycles all over the organization.

Leaders should also Learn

Liu: You advocate teaching organizations and people like Peter Senge advocate learning organizations.

Tichy: That's why Digital Equipment is dead. It was one of the examples of what happens with learning organizations when they aren't teaching organizations.

Liu: But we all know about organizational learning, and nobody uses the term "organizational teaching," which I think is what you are supporting.

Tichy: Right, I spend my life actually doing it. At Royal Dutch Shell there are 70,000 people right now getting taught by their leaders; at Ford 40,000 people; at ATMI, this small hi-tech organization, and at Hewlett-Packard . . . but 90 percent of companies around the world don't do it.

Liu: But you are adding a learning component to your teaching organization idea. In *The Cycle of Leadership*, you said that in *The Leadership Engine* you had missed something; that is, that teachers should also learn.

Tichy: Exactly. As I wrote in *The Cycle of Leadership*, Eckhard Pfeiffer at Compaq was a one-way teacher. He was a brilliant man who did not seem to understand that he would have been smarter and his people smarter if he had been more open to learning. The people in his organization would have bought in more and aligned around executing his strategy. So you can be an autocratic teacher and ultimately fail because in today's world you need to be learning from people down in the organization.

Liu: So actually to me it is like both a teaching and learning organization, right?

Tichy: I would put it this way: A learning organization is the foundation to becoming a teaching organization. You have continuous learning, and then I want you to have the responsibility to teach it to others and begin the virtuous teaching cycle. So you get smarter. It kind of feeds on itself.

Storytelling in Leadership

Liu: You are one of the first people who drew my attention to the role of storytelling in leadership.

Tichy: That was from Howard Gardner.

Liu: I love the idea of the three types of leadership stories. That is very helpful and useful. But when I read your book, I have the impression that you define a story in a very broad sense. To me, some of them are not stories. They are just some adjectives or metaphors.

Tichy: That would not be my definition. Stories are narratives. Howard Gardner once said there are multiple stories. There is the "Who am I?" story. If you look at people like Gandhi, there is a kind of narrative of their lives. There is the "Who we are" story, which is a story about how we are connected and part of something. And then there is the "Where we are going" story, like "We are going to cross the river" or "We are going to climb the mountain."

How do you give your team a sense of identity? Obviously you have to tell a story about the future. I think A. G. Lafley at P&G is developing a very complex movie of the future or writing a novel of the future of P&G in his mind. He can visualize where P&G will be two years from now. He can play that movie in his mind.

I think that's good leadership. That's how I think stories play a key role. It's based on that story line for the future that you make judgments. Then you can decide which people should be on this team or not because this is where the movie is going. The strategy decisions—Should we make this acquisition or not? Should we move into these markets or not?—are based on where we are, how we are moving forward. The story line also prepares me when there's a crisis. Is what I'm doing with this crisis consistent with where we are headed?

Liu: What are the major components of a story?

Tichy: The story line for the organization is the case for change, where we are going, and how we are going to get there. To me those are the three building blocks. If I'm going to mobilize GE, I will say: "Hey, the stock price is down, the world is upset with it. We have to change. Here's where we are going. Here's a picture of what we are going to look like: hi-tech; new technologies; globalization . . . Here are the steps we are going to take: we are going to grow in China this way, we are going to grow in India that way." That's what I think Jeff Immelt is doing.

Liu: What's the difference between a story and an analysis here?

Tichy: The difference is that the story is painting a picture, a script, showing what the play looks like, who the actors are, and what the unfolding themes are, not just a PowerPoint presentation. It's painting a picture.

Jack Welch, the Leader of His Time

Liu: Jack Welch is sort of controversial. There was a cover story in *Fortune*[3] which says "Sorry Jack, your rules are out of fashion" or something like that. And you said that Jack Welch and Alfred Sloan will be the two most remembered and respected business leaders in the twenty-first century.

Tichy: The *Fortune* article was ridiculous. If you look at the so-called new leadership in the article, it's basically Welch leadership. They made up what we call a "straw man" view of Welch. It threw him in with the old command-and-control leadership, which he never was.

Welch started "workout" projects. Welch was engaging thousands of people at all levels in thousands of plants. He was teaching at Crotonville and involving people all the time. That article was a joke.

Liu: What do Jack Welch and Alfred Sloan have in common?

Tichy: They both, in their time, set the stage for what was taught in business schools. Alfred Sloan really was the quintessential manager who created the multi-divisional organization and practiced, in a positive sense, creative scientific management.

All changes have been like a pendulum. Every solution at some point has embodied the next problem. General Motors ultimately became a model for bureaucracy. And that's what Welch inherited at GE too.

Welch really unleashed the human element in the organization, did the best job he could to get rid of bureaucracy, though never totally. He unleashed leadership at all levels in the organization. I think Sloan was a man of his time, and Welch was a man of his time.

I think Jeff Immelt will come up with his answer for the twenty-first century. I don't think he has it yet.

Why Leaders Fail

Liu: You mentioned and praised many business leaders in your book. I have doubts about some of them, like Dick Brown, the former CEO of EDS, who got fired, and also Bob Nardelli, who got fired at Home Depot too. What do you think of those people?

Tichy: I know both of them very well. Dick is a really good guy. He is not a great manager. He doesn't always pay attention to the details.

Liu: He is a great leader but not a great manager?

Tichy: Well, I think to be a great leader you also have to be a good manager. He had certain elements of leadership. But he didn't have the building blocks. So things were out of control.

Nardelli is a little different. Nardelli is a very tough manager, like Welch was. But Welch also had the ability to build people up. Nardelli just uses a hammer. He got away with that at GE, because the organization was strong enough to take some pretty strong leaders and be resilient at the same time. As CEO at Home Depot, he was transforming it and driving very hard. I think he lost touch with the people side of the organization. We saw what happened.

Liu: Jack Welch wrote in his autobiography that when he told the two unsuccessful CEO candidates, one got very mad. I guess that was Nardelli.

Tichy: That was Nardelli. I know all these guys really well. Jim McNerney said, "Well, I would've loved to get it. But life goes on. I get a lot of opportunities." I saw Nardelli three years later and he was still asking "Why not me? Why not me?"

Liu: Another person I have doubts about is Larry Bossidy. He co-authored a book, *Execution*, with Ram Charan, which sold very well in China. He was CEO at Honeywell but, after he retired, Honeywell did not do well and he had to go back. That is not evidence of a great leader to me. What's your comment?

Tichy: I know Larry very well. I think Larry did a number of things. In Allied Signal, he did turn the company around. He ended up merging it with Honeywell, which didn't have a leadership pipeline that was deep enough. Could he have done a better job developing leaders? Maybe. But he was only there for 10 years, and building a leadership pipeline really needs years and years. By the way, Larry came back in and his solution was to bring in David Cote, a former GE leader, from outside and he has done very well.

Larry did not produce CEO candidates for his job. Is he someone who develops leadership? Yes. Did he put a lot of leadership programs together at Allied Signal and Honeywell? Yes. Why didn't he ultimately have the candidate inside the organization? I'm not sure. Maybe he never had enough time. Or he made some mistakes. The reality is, David Cote was brought in from outside.

Building a Leadership Pipeline

Liu: You are saying 10 years is not enough to build the leadership pipeline.

Tichy: When I work with an organization on the leadership pipeline, I'm talking about a people from 22-year-old off-campus hires to the next CEO: the phases you go through from individual contributor to first-time leader, to functional leader, to head of a function, to head of a business.

Liu: That's more like 20 years, then.

Tichy: Yes.

Liu: That's bad news for Chinese companies. Everything in China is going so fast, and they just earn money so easily in many cases. So they don't invest in developing leaders. But now even if they are facing a difficult time, they are dumbstruck by the idea that they have to develop leaders for 20 years to get the results they want.

Tichy: I'll give you one example that's even more interesting. We are working with an organization in Dubai. They have to go from having thousands of employees to 120,000 employees in the next three years. They have decided to build the leadership pipeline without outside hires, which is even more challenging than in China.

There's no easy answer except that the senior leadership has got to put in more time and energy. Whether it is fast enough or not, you have to start.

Liu: And you are saying that the CEO should be the head teacher.

Tichy: Absolutely. If not, it's not going to happen.

Liu: What happens if the CEO is not good at teaching? He may have developed some teachable viewpoints, but lacks the necessary delivery techniques.

Tichy: For leaders who sincerely want to develop themselves in teaching people, we can give them the techniques. Are they going to be world-class teachers? No, they don't need to be. Will they have different personality styles? Yes, of course.

Learning from Welch

Liu: A couple of years ago, I wrote an essay called "What to Learn from Welch." It said that CEOs in China were learning wrong things from Jack Welch—learning to be No. 1 or No. 2, or to fire the bottom 10 percent, or Six Sigma. However, the first thing you should learn is to develop teachers in your organization. You had first-hand experience of how Jack Welch led GE and concluded that he was a world-class teacher. Could you share more?

Tichy: He absolutely understood from day one that the organization would succeed to the extent that it had leaders and was committed to developing as many leaders as possible. I think we are all products of our background. Welch grew up as a working-class kid. As he grew up, he was always putting a team together. He was captain of the hockey team in high school. His view of the world was that you win by building a team.

The GE he took over was a huge bureaucracy. The paradoxical part was that while he was downsizing, he was also investing and developing leaders in the future. For example, when I was running Crotonville, we were building a US$45 million residence facility there. While we were doing that, we were laying people off. People would ask: How can you justify that? And Welch's answer was: "That's about tomorrow. That's about leaders we have in the twenty-first century. We are doing what we have to do to keep our business vital today. We are also going to invest in the future." That was vintage Welch. He was putting huge investments in Crotonville in the development of people even though he had to do some tough stuff. It turns out he was right.

Liu: You said during the two years you were in charge of Crotonville, he showed up and taught every other week. That's very impressive.

Tichy: The only guy that did better was Roger Enrico at Pepsi, who put in more days and actually ran programs for longer periods. I joked with Welch and sent him a *Fortune* article about what Enrico had done and said to him, "You think you are a player, well, the real Olympic player is Roger." What Welch did was that he shared the article around at GE and said, "You are right. We've got to do more teaching."

Liu: Was Welch a natural teacher or did he just get better over time?

Tichy: I think both. When I was there, I don't think he was anywhere as good as he ended up in the year 2000. He had led the plastics business, which was 5,000 or 6,000 people—a small business. It wasn't 400,000 people, which was what it was when he started as CEO at GE in 1981. Back in the plastics days, he had invested a lot in developing and coaching people. What he had to learn was how to do it on a huge scale. You have to rely on other leaders. You can't do it all yourself. I think he learnt that over time. Plus in the 1980s, he had to do some tough things: downsizing, divesting, and so on. That's the learning journey he took.

Liu: Looking back at those leaders you have worked with or had the chance to observe closely, would you still say Jack Welch is the greatest?

Tichy: Absolutely. There are some other very good ones: Jorma Ollila at Nokia, Roger Enrico at Pepsi, David Novak at Yum! Brands, McNerney at Boeing, and Mark Hurd at HP. But it's like going back to Alfred Sloan. At the time, he set the standard. Welch clearly set the standard in his time. He probably was managing one of the most complex companies in the world. So he has been impacting so many different industries. He has been producing more leaders as well, even though they don't all succeed, like Nardelli. There must be 25 or 30 ex-GE people running big companies. Nobody has that record. It happened because Welch focused on leadership.

Liu: And that might be an argument for companies that don't develop leaders. They can steal from GE or Pepsi.

Tichy: I think Welch's answer would be this: "The pyramid shapes this way. So I train as many athletes as I can, but I can only send three to the Olympics. That doesn't mean I stop the pipeline. If I want to win the Olympics I have to keep getting more and better, even if some of them are going to some other places."

Endnotes

1 "Survey: Coming and Going," *The Economist*, October 25, 2003.
2 As we saw earlier, Lafley remained as CEO at P&G until June 2009.
3 Betsy Morris, "The New Rules," *Fortune*, July 24, 2006.

CHAPTER 6

Jerry Porras:
Success Built to Last

Jerry Porras is the Lane Professor Emeritus of Organizational Behavior at the Graduate School of Business at Stanford University. He is the author of *Stream Analysis: A Powerful Way to Diagnose and Manage Organizational Change* (1987) and co-author of two bestsellers: *Built to Last: Successful Habits of Visionary Companies* (1994) and *Success Built to Last: Creating a Life That Matters* (2006).

What is the secret of companies that have achieved enduring success? Jerry Porras, together with Jim Collins, his friend and colleague at Stanford, spent six years, studying 18 "visionary companies," and provided the answer in the bestselling business classic *Built to Last*.

Then how about individuals who have achieved enduring success? Porras and his two co-authors spent 10 years studying more than 200 people who had had a significant impact (and not necessarily in the business sphere) for at least 20 years, and revealed their secrets in another bestseller, *Success Built to Last*.

My conversation with Porras at his Stanford office in June 2008 went the other way round. We started at personal success and ended with organizational leadership.

Redefining Success

Liu: In *Success Built to Last*, you and your co-authors selected successful people to study. How would you define success in the first place?

Porras: That's a good question because it was one of the early and most important findings in this research. If you look up "success" in Webster's Dictionary, it is defined as "the achievement of wealth, fame, or power." That's the generally-accepted view of what success is. We found in the individuals we studied that success is not defined that way. It is defined more in terms of making a difference, making a significant contribution that is important to you and that is lasting.

So we were interested in finding people who made a difference in the world in various ways and at various levels. There are people who have made a difference at the world level and national level—people like, Nelson Mandela and Jimmy Carter, for example—but also people you've never heard of, who have made a difference at the community level or company level.

It was difficult to identify this group in any rigorous sort of way. So we relied on the varieties of lists of "The Most Important People," leaders in industries, and so on. Then we just became opportunistic. One of the co-authors, Mark Thompson, was a very frequent attendant at the World Economic Forum. So he would interview people that went to that.

In deciding what kind of people to interview, our definition of success was based on the notion of having had an impact. It didn't mean they were wealthy or necessarily famous. But they had had an impact for at least for 20 years.

Liu: Even a negative impact?

Porras: Well, we tended to shy away from the negative-impact individuals. You know Osama bin Laden has had an impact. We wouldn't make an attempt to interview him.

Liu: Do you think he is successful?

Porras: In his own terms, I think he thinks he is successful. There certainly are a lot of people who think bin Laden has been very successful and who admire and respect him. I'm not in that camp. So here is where we started to move from purely objective research and scientific orientation to human nature and personal values and beliefs. We have to define and determine what success we are going to admire and what success we are not. That's where our own personal values and our own personal views of the world begin to factor in.

Liu: The definition of success is very important for us. You can try to look at it in an objective way, but it's a tricky concept, a bit like happiness. To the outsider, it may seem that a person is successful or happy, but the person himself may not feel that way.

Porras: Exactly.

Liu: You are talking about people who actually are on some important lists or at a very high position. Other people can see them and know about them. I just met a cleaner outside the building before I came in. He might say, "I feel I'm successful." Would you agree with him?

Porras: Yes. I think the key difference in the way Webster's defines success and the way the individuals we studied define success is that success is very much internally driven. So if the cleaner feels that he is accomplishing something that is important to him and that he thinks he makes a difference and makes an important contribution, and he feels he is doing really well, then he can define himself as successful and be absolutely correct, from our perspective.

Liu: But you are not going to interview him anyway. So there is still an external metric or a set of external metrics you use to judge success.

Porras: Yes, there's no question about that. We did not interview the cleaner but the empirical question still is: if we did, would we find that the way he built his life was similar to the way these people built their lives? That's the ultimate question and the answer we are suggesting is that it would be.

There are individuals we interviewed who are not really well known or who haven't made a lot of money. But in fact they really had an impact in the universe in which they operated. I like to use the example of Norma Hotaling, a drug addict and prostitute in San Francisco. She got herself out of prostitution, stopped being an addict and then built a community organization that helps women like her get out of similar situations. At the time we interviewed her, she wasn't famous. Most people in San Francisco didn't know who she was. But people in the community that she was helping certainly knew. She had been making a big difference for at least 20 years, another of the criteria we used.[1]

Liu: I regularly facilitate a workshop for Chinese managers on the subject of how to manage and lead yourself. In that workshop I say, "Don't pursue success. Pursue achievement." And they ask, "What's the difference?" I say that achievement is what you have done, and success is what the world . . .

Porras: . . . thinks you have done.

Liu: Right. You may or may not get fame, money, or position. But don't worry about that.

Porras: In the language of this book, the way we would say it is "pursue your passion," which is not quite "pursue achievement," but involves achievement. In order for you to pursue your passion successfully, you have to achieve something. The key ingredient is that you are achieving in an area that is very important to you.

The example you gave earlier about people being very wealthy, very famous, yet very unhappy, I think is a product of what they have achieved or not achieved in their passion. If they are achieving their passion, I don't think they are unhappy. That's what the data seem to tell us.

The Road to Success

Liu: Actually, I was about to get on to the question of "passion." I have borrowed some ideas and stories from your book in my workshop. For me, a very important message from the book is that passion should be the fundamental drive of our lives. Did this finding surprise you?

Porras: It did a bit. It surprised us because we were sort of embedded in the classical definition of success in which there is no mention of passion. That passion was such a powerful force and that it was the key determinant to whether people feel successful or not, that was a bit of surprise.

However, it wasn't a total surprise, because the findings in *Built to Last* had already shown us that those companies that lived their values and pursued a fundamental purpose beyond maximizing profits wound up being more significant in the world. They wound up being more admired in the world. They wound up performing better economically too. That was a paradoxical finding. So the parallel at the individual level is that if you pursue your purpose, which one could say is parallel to passion, and you do it well, then you will be more successful in a lot of ways, even in the traditional ways, than if you pursue being successful in those traditional ways.

Liu: The book says that the intersection of three circles—meaning, thought and action, respectively—defines enduring success. What happens to people who only have two circles, say, only meaning and thought, or meaning and action, or thought and action?

Porras: Well, you get different types of results with those different combinations. So people who have meaning and thought would be passionate about something. They would think about it in ways that could supposedly satisfy their passion, but they would take no action.

Liu: They're always talking.

Porras: You're exactly right. But without the action, it's just talk. So those individuals will probably wind up being frustrated in never having achieved anything tangible. They will be like dreamers. They'll be dreaming about "I'll do this," "I'll do that," but never actually doing it.

If we have people who have meaning and action, their outcome is a bit different. They are achieving things but they'll probably have difficulty achieving those things more because they don't have the mental set necessary to really continue to achieve. For example, learning from mistakes is a thought style. If they don't have that capacity, they will make mistakes and keep making the same mistakes over and over again. So the level of accomplishment of whatever passion they are trying to fulfill will probably be lower. But they will be getting things done, whereas the first group will not.

Now, to have thought and action, and not meaning, is to be all over the place. You take this action, get something done and maybe feel good about it but it won't have a lasting effect because it isn't fulfilling any passion. Some other opportunities, some other challenges will come up and you will jump in. So what we will probably see is a life in which a person has done a lot of different things but never really made substantial, meaningful, enduring contributions because they are all over the map.

Liu: So the circle of meaning is pretty much the circle of passion.

Porras: Right. What your passion is about, what the most important thing is in your life, what you would do without getting paid for it, what makes you get excited when you get other people to follow you in accomplishing; that's what meaning is all about.

Liu: I also use three circles in my workshop, which are a little different from yours. I got this from Jim Collins, and it is parallel to the hedgehog concept in *Good to Great*.[2]

Porras: His three circles are what your passion is about, what you can be world class at, and what drives your economic engine.

Liu: And mine are passion, strength, and opportunity.

Porras: What Jim found in *Good to Great* was a way of converting the concept of "big hairy audacious goals" into a concrete reality. His three circles are a way of operationalizing those goals, which was what we discovered in the *Built to Last* study.

Learning from Failure

Liu: The next question is about learning from failure, or learning from mistakes, which you just touched on earlier. In *Success Built to Last* you say that "builders," or enduringly successful people, learn from failure. It's not a big secret that people should learn from their failure. So why don't people do that? Do you have advice on how to learn from failure?

Porras: To answer the first part of your question—why people don't learn from their failure—I think there is an incredible amount of defensiveness in most people and the defensiveness revolves around learning to maintain a certain image, a certain stature with your peers and everybody around you. So if you fail at something, it is negative information about your confidence, your judgment, your intelligence, or whatever. People feel they need to protect their self-image. As a result they are defensive about the failure. How they handle it is typically to try to, as we say in the US government, put a spin on the failure so that it doesn't look like a failure. Or they try to cover it up, which is another thing we see a lot in government and business.

So the more people lack confidence in themselves, the more likely they are to be defensive. If they have more confidence in themselves and their abilities, the less likely they are to be defensive and the more able to analyze and assess the failure and move from there to learning from it. Now what can be done? There are in my mind two ways of thinking about that question. One is the individual in isolation and the second is the individual in an organization.

Liu: Could you explain?

Porras: Let me first talk about the second, the individual in the organization. The organization can create an environment in which a failure is punished or judged or there is some negative reaction to it. In that circumstance, no matter how strong their ego or self-confidence, people are likely to try to hide failures.

In contrast, an organization can be one that values failures, like 3M. 3M makes it possible for people to publicly describe and detail their failures. In our research for *Built to Last*, I talked to the inventor of Post-It notes and he described in detail what had happened. It was a really powerful example of an individual who had failed in accomplishing a particular project to create a kind of glue, but who could openly talk about it in a public setting.

When I teach this in executive programs, I ask the executives, "How many of you have had the opportunity to stand in front of 30 or 40 of your peers and spend an hour going into minute detail describing a failure you are responsible for?" Your culture may be different, but in the United States, in Western cultures, almost nobody raises their hand. In fact, they laugh about it.

Liu: It's probably the same in China.

Porras: So you don't talk about failures openly. At 3M the organization is structured and procedures are put in place to make these discussions happen so that someone else may learn something from it. The Post-It is a great example of someone sitting in the audience, hearing this, and figuring out there might be another application of the failed glue. And that failure became the most successful product 3M ever had.

So, organizations can create cultures, systems, procedures, and policies that reinforce open discussion and learning from failures. Even people who might be defensive about their failures are overpowered by an environment in which it's OK to talk about it. So the environment can make a very substantial difference in the behavior of the individual. If one is thinking about enhancing the learning from failures, I think the very first place to focus on is the organization in which the person is supposed to be learning from failures.

Now if we think about individuals, independent of organizations—which is harder to do because most of the things people do are in the context of an organization—part of the process is a mind game that the person has to play with himself or herself about a failure. Part of the mind game is asking and exploring questions within yourself, such as, "What is the worst thing that could happen if I talk about this failure, if I don't hide it, if I don't react like it didn't happen?" When you look at that, often the worst thing that could happen is not very scary. It's not clarifying the worst thing that's scary. It's the ambiguity that's scary. So one way that people could start to manage themselves out of that is through asking themselves those sorts of questions.

A second way to think about it is delivering the idea in educational experiences like the one you are offering, promoting failures as opportunities for learning. Most of us don't grow up with that idea. Most of us grow up with the idea that failures are bad. So there is a self-analysis and self-managing process, but also an external educational process. The education can also involve real examples like the Post-It of how a failure was learned from and created great success.

Two Types of Leader

Liu: In an interview, you once said that before you and Jim Collins did research for *Built to Last*, you both had the idea that it took a great leader to create and lead a great company. How did the research change that idea?

Porras: Basically, it changed our view of what a great leader is.

Before we started the research, Jim and I were having lots of conversations about organizations. I was saying what really guides an organization is purpose. He was saying what really guides an organization is mission. So we were back and forth. Are they the same? Are they different? This slowly evolved into thinking about doing some research together and we thought it would be good to learn more about great organizations and how they got to be great.

We then had a very simple model: we said it takes great leaders to build great organizations. It's not an outrageous statement, I think. Then we asked ourselves what makes a great leader. We were having this discussion in the late 1980s, when much management thinking in the US about leadership revolved around leaders having to be visionary.

Liu: That was when Iacocca was an icon.

Porras: Exactly. He was considered a visionary leader and he was the ideal model. He was the poster child at that time. Everybody said, "This is a great leader and he is very visionary."

When we looked for the definition and description of a visionary leader, one of the words that showed up in almost every account was "charismatic." In order to be a great leader, you had to be charismatic, brilliant, insightful, committed, focused, risk-taking . . . It took all those things to be visionary.

We then said, if it takes a great leader to build a great organization, and a great leader is a visionary leader, and a visionary leader is charismatic, who are the great charismatic leaders of organizations that we think are great? The first organization that popped into our minds was 3M. But when we began to explore a little bit, we couldn't find a leader at 3M, from the founders forward, who met that description of a visionary leader. We could find no one who was that charismatic. We found very successful, effective leaders but none of them could be typified as "charismatic."

Because our little theory had broken down, we decided that maybe we had put the spotlight on the wrong entity and that, instead, we ought to focus on the great organizations, rather than on visionary leaders, and ask how they were built.

It turned out when we studied these organizations, they had great leaders but the great leaders were defined in a different way. It turned out that style was not the important characteristic. Whether you are charismatic or not isn't important, because virtually none of the great leaders in visionary companies was charismatic.

What we found was that the great leaders in the visionary companies focused on building great organizations. The great leaders in the comparison companies, who by and large were generally charismatic, focused on *leading* their organizations, which means that they created companies that depended heavily on them to be successful. They depended on their brilliance as technologists, as strategists, as advertisers, as product developers, as financial geniuses, and so on.

Liu: In *Built to Last*, there is a beautiful metaphor for this: time-tellers as opposed to clock-builders.

Porras: That's exactly right. Those who focused on leading the organization were the time-tellers, while those who focused on building a great organization were the clock-builders. That was the most significant difference between the two sets of leaders. If you want to build an enduringly great organization, you have to focus on just that. If you want to build an organization that is just successful when you are there, you don't care very much about what it's like after you are gone, then you build an organization that is dependent on you. If you are brilliant enough, it will be very successful. And these comparison organizations were very successful while the great leaders were there. After the great leaders left, these great organizations didn't die, but they never achieved the same levels of success.

Liu: What did those leaders focus on to build the clock?

Porras: This wasn't something they learned externally, because most of the organizations we studied were founded in the 1930s or earlier. There wasn't a lot of information being exchanged at that time. There weren't a lot of books being written about management. They were following these paths intuitively and what we found was that across 18 of these companies, there were some similar activities being pursued. I likened it to 18 people who were all inventing the wheel independently of each other. They all invented pretty much the same wheel.

That wheel is what we call a "visionary organization." It needs to have a core ideology; it needs to have a passion for change; it needs to have processes that preserve the core ideology and that stimulate change. And we describe the six common mechanisms for preserving the core and stimulating change. So if you build an organization, you would be asking yourself, "Does my organization have these characteristics?"

Liu: These are actually the core findings of the *Built to Last* research.

Porras: Let me add in some dimensions to make it more concrete. We say we build an organization that has these mechanisms and these characteristics. But how do we convert that to the very concrete working organization? So here is where some other work I have been doing starts to fit in and give some answers. The answers lie in thinking about what it is in the organization that affects behavior.

To have an effective organization, we have to have effective behavior on the part of the people that work in the organization. There is a social cognitive theory which basically says that there are factors in the environment that drive behavior and will mostly explain behavior. If we are going to understand why people behave the way they do in a work setting, we need to understand the environment they are in.

So the environment has to be conceptualized. The concept that I have used is that there are four main arenas in the work environment. The first is what I call the organizing arrangements—the structure, the policies and procedures, the formal systems that exist. The second category is what I call social factors, and here we have the culture of the organization, the informal networks of communication and influence, the leadership style, and so on. The third dimension is what I call the technology, and here we have the machinery and equipment people work with, the designs of the jobs, the technical systems such as scheduling systems and the exchange of technical information, and so on. The final dimension is the physical setting. Whether we have offices with long halls and closed doors, whether we have open bullpens, whether we have a factory that's dirty or dark or clean, and so on.

So those four arenas send signals to people about behavior. Now these ideas and the *Built to Last* ideas merged in that we want to design those arenas in such a way that they are consistent with the core ideology and they continue to stimulate change. So if we design a structure, is that structure consistent with the ideology? If we have a reward system within that formal structure, is that reward system consistent with the value system? Do they serve the purpose? If we ask that question about each of the four arenas, we can then begin to build an environment that is aligned to deliver signals that are consistent around behaviors that we want. *Built to Last* is a photograph of an ideal organization. How do we translate that photograph into much more concrete reality? I would suggest that it is by recognizing these four arenas and asking the question: what should they look like to be consistent with this picture?

Organizational Architect

Liu: People like you usually have their favorite name for their favorite type of leader. Jim Collins, for example, has Level 5 Leaders; or Bill George has Authentic Leaders. Do you have a name for your favorite type of leader?

Porras: Yes. I call them "Organizational Architects."

Liu: Could you explain that a little?

Porras: What I just described for you are, in essence, the components of the architecture of an organization. The idea is that a leader needs to consciously build the organization in such a way that it promotes the behaviors of the people in the organization that make the organization successful, but also the behaviors that help the individual to develop and grow. So it's a dual bottom line.

We want to have a more successful organization, and we also want to have more developed people. If the two happen, then you can get long-term organizational success and an enduring organization. If you only get organizational success but you don't get the individual development, that success will be temporary. If you get just individual development but not organizational performance, that development will also be temporary. So having both guarantees the long-term, enduring nature of the organization. Just like an architect builds a building, an organizational architect builds an organization.

Liu: You were highlighting the vitality of developing people. I would like to talk a little more about it. In management theory, people have been viewed differently over time: as costs, as human resources, as human capital. What's your view about that?

Porras: The evolving view of people reflects the evolving view of how societies conceptualize people. As societies become more humane, our views of individuals in organizations have also become more humane: so people have moved from being just tools of production to being more fully human. We are not totally there yet when there are still a lot of organizations that view people as tools for production.

I think one thing that is universal is that people like to feel they are contributing something that's important—important to them, important to the company, important to the country, and important to the society. I believe also that people intrinsically like to do a good job. I think that you have to be psychologically ill to have the perspective that you are going to work today and mess up, create problems, fail, and do a bad job.

Liu: You think people go to work and want to do a good job?

Porras: I think in most cases people just go to work. They don't think so much about the job they are going to do because the organization continues to not value the job that they do or the contribution they make. But I think given a free choice, people would rather go to work, contribute something that's important, feel that they are contributing something that's important, and get feedback and rewards that tell them that what they contributed is important. I think almost everybody would rather exist in such a situation, rather than one in which they are looked upon as a cost, as being lazy, as a failure, or as incompetent.

So, if we believe in that assumption we need to change the focus of what the organization does in relation to people. This is where the idea of development begins to fit in. If you believe people want to do a good job, then why not try to create an organization to make it possible? If all that becomes possible and people behave accordingly, then you tend to have a much higher-performing organization.

In our evolution in how we see people, we get closer and closer to seeing them in this humane way. But we are not there yet. I don't know enough about organizations in China, but my speculation is that a substantial number of organizations, especially in the production facilities, still view people as milk cows and wheels and they are to be told what to do.

Liu: I agree with you that we are not there yet. Because whether you treat people like costs, or resources, or capital, you still don't treat people as people.

Porras: Exactly. That's very well put. If you don't treat people as people, they don't act like people.

Liu: My colleagues and I are writing a book with the working title "Treating Employees as People." Not as capital or resources, but as people.

Porras: That's right. You make decisions about them that do not enhance their willingness to work hard and produce. So, if they are part of capital or resources, you feel free to reduce them and kick them out. So United Airlines kicked out thousands of people. What about the 200,000 that are left? Many of them are afraid they might be next. Many more would behave in ways just to protect their jobs and not necessarily think about doing a good job for the company. There's an old saying here in the US, pay me now or pay me later.

Liu: What does that mean, exactly?

Porras: It means sooner or later you have got to pay. You will not be able to avoid paying a price to get out of a difficulty. You can choose to pay that price now or later, but the price has to be paid.

Purpose Beyond Profit

Liu: I would like to move on to some questions about purpose. There has long been a debate over the purpose of a company. I think most business people, whether in the US or China, still are not convinced that a company should have a purpose beyond profit. Does this disappoint you?

Porras: No. I think it's a reality. I think what we have to do is distinguish between making a reasonable profit and maximizing profits. You've got to make a profit otherwise you don't survive. That's just the reality. Being unprofitable is not a feasible option. The choice is between making a reasonable profit and maximizing profits.

Now the economist's view of the world is that organizations exist to maximize shareholders' wealth, which means maximizing profits. That's been the heritage of thinking in the economic world. So it's no wonder that that's how most managers think.

Our findings in *Built to Last* were very profound in this regard, in that they show that those companies that focused on maximizing profits over a 70-year period performed better than the market by a factor of 3:1. But, in comparison, those companies that focused on pursuing their purpose performed better than the market by 15:1. I updated the data to year 2000, 10 years later, and found that the visionary companies had performed better than the market by 16:1. The others also went up, to 4:1, but the visionary companies are still continuing to improve.

The data are pretty powerful but people just refuse to accept them. They somehow continue to claim that there is something wrong with the analyses or that it's just a freak aberration or whatever. They don't want to let go of the idea that the only way to make a lot of money is to focus on maximizing profits. I think people don't want to let it go because it's easier not to.

It's easier to focus on that. It's clear. Everybody knows about it. You are not getting many complaints about it. People aren't going to criticize you for it because it's well accepted. But to say, "Our focus is to make the contribution that's implied in our purpose and if we do that really well, we are going to make a lot of money. We are not going to focus on making a lot of money. We are going to focus on serving our purpose," takes more courage and is a harder sell than to say we are going to focus on maximizing shareholders' wealth.

A More Complex View of Vision

Liu: You mentioned earlier that you and Jim Collins had some debate over whether it was purpose or mission that drives a company. Could you differentiate between purpose and mission?

Porras: "Purpose" is not commonly used, but "mission," "vision" and "values" are. My perspective from the research is that these terms are often used in multiple ways.

Mission is sometimes used to describe a contribution you want to make. If you use it that way, it's more like purpose. But sometimes mission is used to describe what you are doing: "Our mission is to provide health care to the Northern California community." That's a description of what you are doing. Sometimes mission is the responsibility that you have. For instance, the military might say, "Our mission is to protect the northern sector." And sometimes mission, is a big goal you want to achieve. "Our mission is to land a man on the moon and get back by the end of the decade." The word can be used in those four contexts, so when you use the word "mission," I don't know which meaning you intend until I listen more and find out.

Purpose has a much more definite, narrow meaning—it relates to why you exist and the fundamental contribution you make. That's why we used "purpose" rather than "mission."

When we were starting our discussions, we weren't very clear about those differences. We were also coming from working with different groups. Jim had been working with management teams from small companies, for whom mission was much more a major goal. I had been working with larger organizations as a whole. Jim was a consultant, and I was thinking theoretically. I was trying to figure out the glue that holds organizations together; what defines what the structure looks like, the culture, and all that. I was thinking of the word "purpose" as being the glue that holds things together because if everybody understands the purpose, then you design the structure in a culture, technology and physical setting to be consistent with the purpose to help you achieve the purpose. So we were coming from very different places in the way we were thinking about the words we were using. And that's the reason we had a disagreement. But out of discussions we began to understand each other better.

Liu: How about values and vision?

Porras: When people talk about values, they can be core values, which were the ones we discovered in our research. They are unchanging, small in number—maybe three to five—very fundamental. You live them no matter what happens. They are different from the other values in the organization, which I now describe as strategic values—the values the organization adopts in order to implement its strategy. The key thing is if you change the strategy, you should change the values. The reality is that you change the strategy and often the values don't change. That blocks you and your achievement in the new strategy. One of the problems with change is how you change those values. But core values and strategic values are two different types of values that exist in the organization. Core values do not change; strategic values are dynamic and they should change.

Vision is thought about most commonly as a view of the future, or a dream that you have about what the future should be like. If you ask yourself, "What is vision supposed to do for an organization?" and are really serious about this, you could come up with a pretty long list of requirements. Vision is supposed to motivate people, to inspire them, to focus them, to guide behavior, to limit activities, and so on.

I asked executives in executive programs to tell me what they thought vision should do for their company, and we came up with a list of up to 20 items. Then I asked them, "Does your company have a vision?" And they all raised their hands. Then I asked them, "Among all these items written on the board, how many of them are satisfied by your company's vision?" Usually the answer was three to five; which means 15 to 17 items were not satisfied by their company's vision.

So what's wrong? It is that the traditional view of vision is not complex enough. That's where we came up with the description of vision in *Built to Last*, which is that vision is more complicated than just a dream of the future. So if you want to satisfy all those 20 items, you have to be much more complex.

If you look at what the visionary companies are doing to satisfy all of the 20 items, first of all, they have a purpose that satisfies some of the items; then they have core values that satisfy another set of items; and they also have a big hairy audacious goal that satisfies the remaining items. These three things together will satisfy all those 20 items. So vision is these three things. Plus, you have to communicate it. If you've got them, then you've got vision.

Endnotes

1 Norma Hotaling died of pancreatic cancer on December 16, 2008, at the age of 57.

2 Jim Collins uses "the hedgehog concept" to advocate that a company should focus, rather than diversify, as the contrast between the hedgehog and the fox (see "The Fox and the Hedgehog" box in Chapter 2). In his book *Good to Great: Why Some Companies Make the Leap . . . and Others Don't* (Harper Collins, 2001), Collins argues that a company, in order to leap from good to great, is required to have a deep understanding of the intersection of three circles: what it is deeply passionate about, what it can be the best in the world at, and what drives its economic engine. The good-to-great companies translate the understanding into a simple, crystalline concept—the hedgehog concept—and stick to it.

Leading Through Storytelling

CHAPTER 7

Howard Gardner: Leaders as Storytellers

Howard Gardner is the John H. and Elisabeth A. Hobbs Professor of Cognition and Education at the Harvard Graduate School of Education. The author of more than 20 books, translated into 29 languages, and several hundred articles, Gardner is best known in educational circles for his theory of Multiple Intelligences. He is a member of the American Academy of Arts and Sciences, the American Philosophical Society, the National Academy of Education, and the London-based Royal Society for the Encouragement of Arts, Manufactures, and Commerce. He was twice selected by *Foreign Policy* and *Prospect* magazines as one of the 100 most influential public intellectuals in the world. In May 2008, he was ranked the fifth-most influential business thinker by *The Wall Street Journal*.

Prior to 2004, Gardner's influence had been largely confined to the fields of psychology and education. In the 1980s, he had come up with the theory of Multiple Intelligences, which challenged the restrictive nature of the traditional IQ test and extended the component features of human intelligence.[1] These ideas have been hugely influential, being applied to all kinds of educational projects around the world.

In 2004, Gardner made his breakthrough as a "public intellectual" with *Changing Minds*. "Changing minds" was a major issue in the US presidential election of that year and Gardner was inundated with requests for interviews from the mass media. He commented later, "Clearly, the serendipity of the book's publication date and the personae of the major candidates combined to make me an instant expert on presidential politics."[2] Clearly, though, there was nothing instant about his expertise: he had been developing his ideas on the human mind for decades.

Gardner first came to my attention a couple of years ago when I read an interview with Noel Tichy, in which Tichy attributed his idea of three types of leadership stories to Gardner, saying, "*Leading Minds* was the big 'aha' for me."[3] This prompted me to research Gardner's ideas in general and those about leadership in particular.

A prolific writer, Gardner has many books to his name. It was his books *The Unschooled Mind* (1991) and *Creating Minds* (1993) that led him to study leadership, culminating in the publication of *Leading Minds* in 1995.

In *Creating Minds*, Gardner studied seven creative people, including Freud, Einstein, Picasso, and Gandhi. As a consequence of writing the book, he realized that Gandhi stood out from the rest as a leader across domains. He was intrigued by this and began to explore what made cross-domain leaders special.

In *The Unschooled Mind*, Gardner had found that people have formed informal theories about the world at the age of five. Those theories are interesting but usually flawed or completely wrong. Even after many years of formal schooling, most adults still think like a five-year old in many respects. This led him to question how a leader, faced with unschooled minds, could communicate effectively. He came up with the answer in *Leading Minds*: stories.

Though triggered by *Creating Minds*, *Leading Minds* has deeper roots; Gardner's lifelong fascination with politics and history, and his belief in leadership. "Much of what is beneficent in the world has been inspired by farsighted leaders," he claimed.

When I finally sat down with Gardner at his Harvard office in October 2008, another US presidential election was reaching its climax, the severest economic crisis since the 1930s was unfolding in the US, and the notorious poison-milk scandal was being exposed in China—a fitting backdrop for a discussion on political and business leadership.

A Cognitive Approach to Leadership

Liu: In *Leading Minds*, you take a cognitive approach to leadership. From a cognitive view, how do you define leadership?

Gardner: Traditionally, leadership has been studied by political scientists and historians. When psychologists first began to study leadership, it was primarily psychoanalysis, studying what kinds of people have the personality to become a leader, and why they become a leader, what needs does it fulfill for the leader and for the audience. They also studied leadership in terms of social psychology: how people persuade others, about attitudes, beliefs, motivations, and so on.

By training, I'm a cognitive psychologist. Cognitive psychology really arrived because of computers. Computers became more than number crunchers; they became tools which could solve problems, maybe even create things. When you can write the rules so specifically that computers can do it, you can say, "Well, we can also write the rules for human beings." That approach wouldn't have been possible 50 years ago because we didn't have computer models.

What cognitive scholars do is rethink terms of mental representations, which means the language of the mind. How does the mind take things in? How does it store them? How does it manipulate them? How does it remember them? How does it misremember them? And so on.

I'm a scholar of mind and intelligence. I'm trained in thinking about the mind. So when I began to study leadership, as a psychologist I naturally looked at people who are very effective leaders. I defined leaders as people who could get other people to do things without forcing them.

Mao Tse-tung is quite interesting in this regard because he would never have gotten to where he did if he hadn't been able to influence people to follow him back in the Long March. On the other hand, by the time he became the supreme leader, he had too much power. Then he just told people what to do; he didn't bother to convince them anymore. So he would be less interesting to me after 1960 than before. He would be more interesting to me in 1930 than in 1956 for the same reason. Stalin, Hitler, and many people who we don't honor in the West would not have gotten to where they did unless they initially had been able to persuade and convince other people.

So I ask myself the question: What are the major tools that leaders have to convince other people to think differently, feel differently, and behave differently? In my later writings, I talked about lots of different kinds of tools. It occurred to me that the leader has to use a tool which he can assume everybody possesses if he wants to lead widely.

What everybody from the age of three or four possesses is that they create and understand stories. All over the world we tell stories to children. They repeat them; they change them; they make them up, and so on. All of us have many, many stories in our minds. Hundreds of them.

So a leader has two challenges. The first challenge is coming up with the story that people pay attention to. If the story is too familiar, it just gets assimilated into the stories we already have. I almost never watch television stories because I know where they are going. They are not very interesting. On the other hand, if the story is too strange, too exotic, too eccentric, people cannot hold on to it. So the first thing the leader has to do is come up with a story which gets people's attention and makes them feel this way: "Yeah! This is very interesting. I haven't thought of this. But I can understand it."

The second thing is that this story has to be embodied in the life that the leader lives and in the way the leader behaves. If I tell one story, but in my own life I lead a very different kind of story, then in the end it doesn't have much power. I can fool people only for a while.

That's the core of a cognitive approach to leadership. You might say it's computer science plus Darwin, because all these stories are competing. In the recent presidential election, there were many stories about Obama and about McCain. And the person that is most effective in getting people to vote for him or her, is the one whose story you can connect with.

That is the interesting thing about the vice presidential candidate Sarah Palin. Around universities we laugh at her because she is so ignorant about international affairs. But she connects to ordinary people. This is the part of democracy that people in China or in Singapore laugh at. Somebody with so little talent and so little knowledge can persuade many people to vote for her. The story she tells, and the story that she embodies, connects to people.

Liu: In *Leading Minds*, you define a leader as "an individual who significantly affects the thoughts, feelings and/or behaviors of a significant number of individuals."

I talked to John Kotter at Harvard Business School and Ronald Heifetz at Harvard Kennedy School. Kotter said "leadership is to mobilize people to make great things happen." Heifetz said "leadership is to mobilize people to face the tough reality and make adaptive change." It seems that all of your definitions have a lot in common: followers and changes. In this respect, the cognitive view doesn't seems that different.

Gardner: It's partly because all of us are part of general intellectual currents which are powerful around the university. But my focus is different. Kotter is not particularly from psychology. Heifetz comes much more from psychoanalysis and personality psychology. So they would not be so interested in what I call mental representation; namely, the way somebody actually hears things, transforms things, and so on.

The Major Form of Stories

Liu: In your view, a leader changes other people's minds through telling stories. But it seems to me that you define "story" broadly.

Gardner: You are correct. I define it very broadly. Stories are a very interesting phenomenon. That is why people all tell stories. Are you married?

Liu: Yes.

Gardner: When you come home and your wife says: "How was the trip?" and you say, "First I went here. Then I went there." She is not going to pay attention. If you say, "When I got to the airport, I suddenly discovered that I had left all my important documents behind," that would get her attention.

Liu: That's narrative. That's the major form of a story. But you also write in *Leading Minds* that the phrases of a sonata and the gestures of a dance are also stories.

Gardner: Let me first go back to narratives. The way I define it, a narrative isn't just one thing after another. Rather, there is some kind of a problem, or obstacle, or puzzle which gets people's interest. Then the story involves how the protagonist deals with that particular problem and the tragedy if they fail. But, you know, in life we'd like to have a better ending than average.

If I talk about a story having to do with music, that is a metaphor. I happen to be very involved in music. There are some musical compositions where the metaphor of narrative is more compelling. Everybody knows Beethoven's Ninth Symphony and all enjoy the last movement. Beethoven specifically developed a bunch of themes and then he rejected them, until he came up with "Dah-Dah-Dah- Dah." [Gardner sings here] That was a real story.

Liu: So you still refer to narratives as stories.

Gardner: Yes. I think it's basically linguistic or something which can be thought of in linguistic terms. In the 1940s, a social psychologist did a very famous experiment. It involved an animated cartoon in which some rectangles, triangles, and circles were moving around. Any ordinary person who looked at that cartoon immediately said, "Oh, it's a boy chasing a girl there." But people who suffer from autism could not see that movie the way ordinary people do. What I am saying here is that you can make a piece of music or a film more like a narrative, but much of music or film doesn't have narratives.

Einstein as a Leader

Liu: Actually in *Leading Minds,* you said a story includes narratives, invented accounts, overt or propositional accounts, and visions of life.

So it seems to me that everything is a story. You also said that Einstein was a leader. His story was not narratives, but ideas of physics.

Gardner: Yes. That's how I got into the idea of leadership. I was not particularly thinking about leadership, which was not a classic problem in cognitive psychology. I was trying to understand creativity. I wrote a book called *Creating Minds*, in which Gandhi was the one most like a leader. I tried to understand what people like Einstein did. I realized they worked with different kinds of symbols: musical symbols, mathematical symbols, and literary symbols. These were very powerful. They did two things: they affected people whom were in contact with them and they changed the way people worked with symbols in the future. After Picasso broke down representational art, people began to open artistic windows and doors which had been closed before.

Eventually when I began to look at leadership, I reconceived creativity in the arts and sciences as what I call "indirect leadership." Those who debate on television or speak in front of large audiences in amphitheaters are direct leaders. It doesn't matter whether people like Einstein or Picasso ever meet anybody else. They write something on paper or its equivalent, and that has a lot of effect.

It's interesting because now the two things are much closer in America; namely, when you write a book, you are expected to go on television and sell the book. If you can't do that, that's a big disadvantage. Now, part of being an "indirect" leader is that you have to become willing to be "direct," go on television and talk about your work. That is indirect leadership being pushed to become more direct.

I'm pretty academic, so when I write a book my publishers would love for me to get arrested for stealing a car so I could be a celebrity on television.

Liu: People like Albert Einstein and Margaret Mead are often referred to as thought leaders. You call them indirect leaders. Are they the same thing?

Gardner: Margaret Mead, a cultural anthropologist, is interesting because more than most of the other indirect leaders, she became a public personality because she happened to be good at it and liked it. To answer your question, yes, I think indirect leaders would be similar except I think most people when they talk about thought leaders will not include artists or inventors. I don't know where the phrase "thought leaders" comes from but we have a phrase now which does apply to me: "public intellectuals." These are people who are basically teachers and writers but who write for something like *The New York Times*, not just for a journal that only specialists read. But a public intellectual is not exactly the same thing as a thought leader. You can be a thought leader whether or not anybody knows what you look like. But for public intellectuals, they know what you look like.

Stories Need to Engage the Audience

Liu: In *Leading Minds*, you said there are three broad categories of stories: stories about the self, stories about the group, and stories about values and meaning.

Gardner: I don't remember that; I wrote the book about 15 years ago. But I believe you!

Liu: Really? That is interesting because this idea has influenced another leadership thinker, Noel Tichy, a lot. He paraphrased that there are three kinds of leadership story: the "Who am I?" story, the "Who are we?" story, and the "Where are we going?" story. Would you agree with him?

Three Types of Leadership Story

Howard Gardner believes that most stories told by leaders are created in response to the pervasive human need to understand better oneself, the groups that exist in and beyond one's culture, and issues of value and meaning. Hence, he delineates stories in three broad categories.

- Stories about the Self: Individuals probe the perennial question "Who am I?" and also look to the leaders for an

(*continued*)

(*continued*)

answer. Although creating a sense of self is a task belonging to the individual himself to a large extent, leaders who help individuals conceptualize a personal identity perform an important function. In 1992, when Bill Clinton presented himself as a "New Democrat," he induced many voters to think of themselves in new and more positive ways.

- Stories about the Group: An individual's sense of identity is largely rooted in his place within various groups. A reflective individual is likely to look for the leader who offers a set of options regarding group membership, including the possibility of creating new groups. For example, the unhappy experience of being a German citizen in punitive post-First World War Europe engendered many political options, including Hitler's new National Socialist Party.

- Stories about Values and Meaning: Particularly in times of crisis or radical change, people pay attention to those who can provide some kind of broad orientation, if not definitive answers to essential questions like the purpose of the work, the value of prayer and other ultimate human concerns. The visionary leader faces the challenge of offering a story that builds on the most credible syntheses of the past, revisiting them in the light of present concerns and leaving open a place for future events, and allows individual contributions by people in the group.

Gardner: If you ask me, "Are they three great and important stories?" my answer is, "Yes, absolutely." If you say, "Are they the only stories?" I would have to think about it.

Liu: When I first heard about the story of the self, I thought it was about the leader himself, in which he let his followers know about him and his values. But I later realized that what you are actually saying is that the leader tells a story that helps the followers identify or find themselves.

Gardner: Absolutely. At least in the contexts which I'm familiar with, the audience has to be able to identify with the story. So the more the story seems exotic, the less they can relate to it. This is one of Obama's problems in running for president. His story is very interesting, but if you are very provincial, if you have never left Montana, the story of his life is not going to have much meaning for you.

So especially in a public setting, the story needs to connect with people at some level. It could be emotional. For example, at the end of the recent vice presidential debate, Senator Joe Biden became tearful because he was remembering his wife who died in an accident. Most people have not had that experience, but we have all had the experience of remembering something that makes us very sad; so people connected there because most people have difficulty hiding their emotions. That's another problem Obama has. He is the most introverted person running for high office in a long time and that makes it difficult for people to get inside him.

Liu: So the story about the self is more about "yourself" than "myself."

Gardner: Let's put it this way. The story that one tells as a leader has to have a mirror in it so that the audience can identify with it. Bill Clinton is the most effective speaker I have ever heard. He could be in a room with thousands of people, and he would be aware of everyone in that room. When he says something that makes some people stiffen up, he picks it up immediately and adjusts his story so that people can feel connected again.

It's the exact opposite of an autistic person. The autistic person says whatever is on his mind and he is pretty much unable to pick up any cues from anybody else.

Leaders Know Themselves

Liu: Let's talk about leadership and multiple intelligences. In *Leading Minds* you highlighted the importance of linguistic intelligence and interpersonal intelligence to leadership. However, you didn't emphasize the importance of intrapersonal intelligence. Many leadership thinkers stress that knowing who you are is very important for a leader. Is the capacity of knowing who you are the same as intrapersonal intelligence? Is it important for a leader?

Gardner: Intrapersonal intelligence and what I would call existential intelligence are certainly very important. I try to make the distinction—and I'm not sure how important it is—between people who analyze themselves and people who are comfortable with themselves. If to know yourself means to know how you are going to react to be effective in certain situations, then I think intrapersonal is very important.

On the other hand, I think most leaders don't have much interest in introspection and trying to understand who they are and what they are doing. Ronald Reagan was a perfect example. Reagan was quite comfortable with himself. I don't think he spent five minutes of his life thinking about motivation or anything like that. That's because leaders are essentially people of action. They spend a little time thinking about things but not a great deal; they think through their actions. I said this in one of the books: Creators, or indirect leaders, spend 90 percent of their time in their own mind, and 10 percent of their time just making sure they are not crazy. Leaders of the direct kind spend 90 percent of their time in interacting with other people, and only 10 percent stepping back, reflecting, and introspecting.

I used to be angry with Bill Clinton because he never seemed to be alone, thinking things through privately. Then I realized that the way he spent time with himself was with other people. Hitler was like this. I think Mao was like this: monologues. They don't particularly care how other people will react. They just would like to have other people around for whatever reason. I think that with Mao, when he became older he became pathological. With Clinton, he just wouldn't like to be alone.

Liu: David Gergen[4] wrote something very interesting about Clinton. He said that Clinton is very clever, he knows what other people want, but he has never known what he wants.

Gardner: As I said in one of my books: Clinton is a great storyteller. He has wonderful stories. But he tells way too many, and it's not clear which one he deeply believes in.

Liu: In the corporate world the theory of emotional intelligence is more popular than the idea of multiple intelligences. My understanding is that, in your framework, emotional intelligence is a combination of intrapersonal and interpersonal intelligences. Do I understand this correctly?

Gardner: Emotional intelligence is basically about understanding yourself and understanding other people. Having intelligence is one thing, but how you use it is quite another. In some of my more recent work in collaboration with Mihaly Csikszentmihalyi and William Damon, I've been looking at applying intelligence for a positive purpose. The Good Work project began in 1994 when the three of us, all psychologists, felt that American society was being undermined and transformed by the prevailing thinking that markets were the best way for running and regulating everything. People were saying government was bad, market was good. We became particularly interested in professions—law, medicine, and journalism—because they have had difficulty surviving as independent institutions with enduring value systems when everything was controlled by the bottom line.

I had never thought much about the professions of accounting or auditing. But in the year 2000 it became clear that auditors were for sale. They gave you the numbers you wanted to have.

Liu: Arthur Andersen?

Gardner: That's right. Now, in 2008, we can see all the costs of unregulated markets. The costs are mostly in the United States and in poor countries, but they are going to have an effect everywhere.

Liu: By good work, I think you refer to work that is excellent, engaging, and ethical. Is that right?

Gardner: That's right, and I would love for these ideas to become better known in China. The reason I think it's important in China is that you have a Confucian tradition, which is thousands of years old, Marxism, which is hundreds of years old (although your Marxism is a kind of Soviet imitation, so it's 80 years old) and then you have the Chinese view of capitalism and markets that started in the 1980s. In combination, they don't work very well, and you end up living in a vacuum, which is not conducive to encouraging excellence, engagement, and ethics and which enables events such as the poisoned-milk episode to occur. When you have an ethical society, people don't poison milk, not simply because they are afraid of what's going to happen to them but also because they are thinking of their ethical responsibilities as a worker or a manager.

Liu: I know your research has covered a broad range of areas, but I have a question specifically about leadership and good work. Intuitively I think a leader's job in an organization is to create and motivate good work. Would you agree?

Gardner: Sure. And the best way to motivate is to embody it yourself and select people who you don't have to train a lot to be that way. Of course it's much easier said than done. You find several people who were glorified in business books in the 1990s are now in jail. So it's much easier to talk the ethics game than to embody it and select people who have ethical DNA. Then the hardest part is to say, "You are great in some ways. But this place is not right for you because you don't get it."

Gardner's Five Minds for the Future

Gardner's newest book, *Five Minds for the Future,* outlines the specific cognitive abilities that will be sought and cultivated by leaders in the years ahead. The comprise:

- The Disciplinary Mind: the mastery of major schools of thought, including science, mathematics, and history, and of at least one professional craft.

(continued)

(*continued*)

- The Synthesizing Mind: the ability to integrate ideas from different disciplines or spheres into a coherent whole and to communicate that integration to others.
- The Creating Mind: the capacity to uncover, and clarify new problems, questions and phenomena.
- The Respectful Mind: the awareness of and appreciation for differences among human beings and groups.
- The Ethical Mind: the fulfillment of one's responsibilities as a worker and as a citizen.

Five Minds for the Future

Liu: I am thinking about the metaphor of the fox and the hedgehog which you also used in your book. It seems to me that you first tell a "story" of multiple intelligences and then you apply it everywhere.

Gardner: Or others do.

Liu: I am also thinking about your recent idea of the five minds for the future, which includes the disciplined mind and the synthesizing mind. Can I say that you became a hedgehog first and then a fox? Or to be effective, profound thinkers should be a hedgehog first and then a fox? And a hedgehog has a disciplined mind and a fox, a synthesizing mind, in your framework?

Gardner: As an academic, I have been struck by how many of my colleagues become interested in something and then they literally study it for 40 years. Within 10 years, they know more than anybody. Sometimes there is 30 years more work to do; and sometimes they just repeat themselves.

The people I most resemble are those who get bored easily. If you get bored easily, you are more inclined to be the fox; that is, to say, "I've done this and I am going to do something else." That's very characteristic of me and the people I most like.

I have said in a few places, "I am a fox that would like to be a hedgehog." That's because I would like to see connections between the various things I do and I get very excited to see the relationship between two things that I am doing which I didn't see at first.

I think that these types—partly cognitive, partly personality—are based in fundamental human psychology. So I don't think you could say people first become a "discipliner," or first become a hedgehog and then become a fox. I went to Harvard College almost 50 years ago and one way in which I stood out among all the students was that I audited more courses than anybody else. That's because I am curious about things. If you last long enough, you can see connections and end up being able to do something that the complete hedgehogs don't do.

Liu: In your recent book, you are turning from description to prescription. You are saying that people should have five minds to be successful in the future.

Gardner: If we are involved in institutions, whether in education or business, these are the skills which we want to cultivate. The last two—respectful mind and ethical mind—have to apply to everyone. The first three— disciplined, synthesizing, and creative minds—are all very important. But like the distinction between the hedgehog and fox, some people are going to be terrific at doing what they do, at their fundamental discipline, but not particularly good at synthesizing.

Liu: So the five minds are more at the organizational level.

Gardner: I think everyone who goes to school ought to be exposed to some manifestations of all five minds. But people would sort themselves out just like hedgehogs and foxes would sort themselves out. I would never be content to be the very best disciplinarian. I am more of a synthesizer. We should help people sort themselves out. It's as wrong to take a highly disciplined engineer from MIT and say "You are to be an entrepreneur" as it is to make somebody who is very broad spend 15 years micro-managing one specific thing. It doesn't work.

Endnotes

1 For details, see Gardner, Howard, *Frames of Mind: The Theory of Multiple Intelligences* (New York: Basic Books, 1983).

2 Howard Gardner, *Changing Minds: The Art and Science of Changing Our Own and Other People's Minds* (Harvard Business School Press, 2006), x.

3 Randall Rothenberg, "Noel M. Tichy: The Thought Leader Interview," *strategy + business*, Spring 2003.

4 David Gergen is a professor at Harvard Kennedy School of Government and the editor of some of Gardner's book. Gergen has served as a White House advisor to four presidents: Nixon, Ford, Reagan, and Clinton.

CHAPTER 8

John Kotter: Stories as a Force for Change

John Kotter is the Konosuke Matsushita Professor Emeritus of Leadership at Harvard Business School. He is widely recognized as one of the foremost authorities in the field of leadership. He has authored or co-authored 17 books, 12 of them bestsellers. He has won many honors, including an Exxon Award for Innovation in Graduate Business School Curriculum Design, a Johnson, Smith & Knisley Award for New Perspectives in Business Leadership, and a McKinsey Award for Best *Harvard Business Review* Article.

He started his teaching career at Harvard Business School in 1972, becoming a full professor in 1980 at the age of 33. When he opted to retire at 54, he quipped that he became the youngest retired professor—after having been the youngest full professor—in his field.

He is, of course, much more than that, being one of the most sought-after gurus in the fields of leadership and change. His name is inherently linked to the term "change leadership," and one of his major messages is "Leadership is about change."

His three most influential books—his "change trilogy"—are *A Force for Change* (1990), in which he differentiated leadership and management as separate activities and processes; *Leading Change* (1996), in which he identified eight steps to successfully leading a change initiative; and *The Heart of Change* (co-authored with

Dan Cohen, 2002), in which he introduced the powerful "see-feel-change" model.

His sixteenth book, *Our Iceberg Is Melting* (co-authored with Holger Rathgeber in 2002), marked a "change" away from his usual academic research work. A fable about how a group of penguins move away from a melting iceberg, the book is consistent with one of his central findings about change, which is that stories are the force for change.

In January 2008, when he was busy writing his next book, *A Sense of Urgency* (published in September that year), we had a dialog starting with the "penguin book" at his home in Cambridge, Massachusetts.

A Different Vehicle for Change

Liu: *Our Iceberg is Melting* is your newest book, I believe?

Kotter: Right.

Liu: When you retired from Harvard Business School a couple of years ago, you said that you were very interested in storytelling. Obviously you have pursued this interest, as this book is a fable and its main characters are penguins. May I ask what's new about the book and how it came about?

Kotter: First of all, it draws content from what we have learned about change. Based on actual research, I published a book called *Leading Change,* which went on to become, at least in North America, the bestselling book on organizational change. We followed up with another book called *The Heart of Change* that went deeper and started telling stories from actual people's points of view.

I was hearing more and more people say, "People belonging to organizations need to understand this material. But most people, except for recent MBA graduates, don't read business books. So what can you do for me?"

At that time I was studying neurology, the study of the brain, trying to understand how people learn in the sense of changing their actions, not just holding information in their brains.

It all seemed to converge at one point when Holger Rathgeber, who is German, sent me an email one day. His idea was to try to put together a story because the brain likes stories. The brain is not built for PowerPoint slides. We decided to write a book that took the same material, expanded it in a few directions, and made it relatively simple and easy, and interesting to read. We put it in a form of a fable. That is what led to the new book.

So, it takes the material from *Leading Change* and *The Heart of Change,* it adds a little bit more about specific personalities, but offers it up in a very different form, with the idea of affecting the brain in a different way and reaching a broader audience. That was the logic behind it.

It was the best-selling business book in Germany for 50 weeks, and Holland for 40 weeks. It's been on one of the charts in America for 16 months. So some people have picked it up. From the emails I get, clearly in some circumstances it is doing what we wanted. People read it. They talk about it. It creates a little language system they don't forget.

Stories remain in the brain, and therefore have some chance of affecting behavior. So it is a different vehicle, a different methodology for helping people with content that I have written about before.

Liu: In other words, it is another way to illustrate your ideas about change.

Kotter: Right. And illustrate them in such a way that the mind can grasp those ideas, hold on to them, and have some chance of changing behavior. I want to help people actually get better results. So performance—individual or organizational—is my field. I am not just writing about it, but trying to help better performance happen.

So, increasingly over the years, the questions that keep going through my mind not only relate to what I observe in the sense of performance, particularly on the leadership side, but how to help people do more than read, nod their head, and then forget. How do you get them to actually somehow absorb material and do something with it? That has affected my writing a lot over the last 15 years. This penguin book was just one more little vehicle for trying to do that.

An Important Tool for Change

Liu: I think this book actually starts from the premise in *The Heart of Change* where you say people should "see, feel, change."

Kotter: Yes.

Liu: In that book you actually outlined many powerful tools for changing behavior, and moving things along, in any of the stages in your eight-step model: a slogan, a picture, a video tape, and so on. So is storytelling just one form of those, or is it the most powerful form?

Kotter: That is a good question, which depends how narrowly or broadly you define or use the word "story." You could define it narrowly, in the sense of "I'll tell you a story about what I did half an hour before you showed up." That is, "I am saying it to you. It is verbal. I could write it down in two or three pages. It is about some kind of event." Yes, that is an important tool.

But you could define it more broadly too. You are experiencing a story right now. The story is the meeting you are having with John. That's the story. You are experiencing it, and the brain is clearly preprogrammed for absorbing that form of "story" because it has been doing this sort of thing for tens of thousands of years. So it is what people call "hardwired" to absorb and retain that form of story.

Another form of story comes through video. I have been using videos in my speeches for years now. They are videos of people and companies and sometimes they stand by themselves as a story and sometimes you have tell an audience what else was happening before or after what they see. This is not a story in the sense of occupying written pages. It's not a verbal speech: grandfather telling the grandchildren a "story." But it can be a very, very powerful way to grab people's attention, give them an idea or two, and leave it in the brain so that it might affect their behavior.

So, if you define a story in broad terms, if it is not the most powerful tool to change behavior that can create better performance, it is certainly close. If you define it narrowly, it is yet one more tool, albeit an important one.

How Managers Use Stories

Liu: I read your essay "The Power of Stories" you wrote for *Forbes* in 2004. I notice that you did not say that CEO should tell stories.

Kotter: I believe I said they usually don't, or aren't very good at it, at least in general.

Liu: Now some people are advocating that CEOs should tell stories. What do you think about it?

Kotter: I do know some CEOs who, as part of the many things they do, are good at telling a little story to illustrate a point, to make an idea more alive, to engage people more, and to have people understand something more clearly than when they say "A causes B, which leads to C." But that is not what I am speaking of here.

I am saying that stories are tools that can be used by anyone and they can come in many forms besides a verbal recital. Stories can be given by somebody like myself, in written form, say in a book. They can also be videotapes that anybody can use. Both are quite independent of a "CEO telling stories." So, do I think CEOs should tell stories? Sure, if they are good at it, but that's just one of many ways that stories can be used to increase performance. Let's not get too carried away with focusing on CEOs talking.

Liu: The two examples you use in your *Forbes* essay are Lou Gerstner and Sam Walton. What I see from these examples is that they didn't tell stories as much as they turned themselves into stories.

Kotter: Very good. That is what I meant by role modeling. That is what I meant by "one of the things you are experiencing right now is the story of your meeting with John." I think those two guys were a little bit more conscious of what they were doing than most, so they were more purposive and effective.

There is an expression in English—I don't know if it is translated into other languages—"Show them, don't tell them." It is very often what great novelists do. They don't say, "George has these six personality characteristics, period." They write in a way that demonstrates it. It's more powerful that way.

Lou Gerstner, for one, is a great example of someone who knows how to show and not just tell. I love the example of his turning off the video projector.[1] That says it all. He created this little story through his actions one day which went out faster, stronger, and clearer than any memo he could ever send out. So yes, I think there are some CEOs who are very good at that—and more could be and should be.

Liu: Now there are workshops to teach managers and CEOs how to tell stories. Do you think that is helpful?

Kotter: In one of our one-week executive programs at Harvard, the facilitators spend a day focusing on helping the participants think about getting better at telling stories. How much value does it have? Honestly, I don't know. I think it helps, but how much I don't know.

Liu: Then should managers and CEOs learn storytelling, or is it OK to leave it to professional people, like trainers in the company?

Kotter: Sure, have them learn, have them use it as a tool, but be clear that a verbal telling of a story by a manager is just one way that stories can be tools to improve performance. Everybody tells stories. Some people tell them more often and better, but everybody tells stories. If a manager is bad at it, and you can give him a little bit of help, and it is not too expensive, it's probably not a bad idea. But having an executive program that is called "Storytelling" and is three weeks long may not be the best way to help people.

Telling a Good Story

Liu: Do you have any advice on how to tell a good story?

Kotter: Using story as a tool—not just "telling a good story"—starts with the content. If you use a story, it has to have a point. What are you trying to achieve? Be clear with that.

I think, obviously, the more engaging the better: interesting, funny, and dramatic. That helps. If there are characters that people can identify with, that helps. Most stories have a beginning, a middle and an end. Structure helps.

I suspect experts on stories know a lot about that. I don't. I haven't dug into it. I haven't analyzed the nature of storytelling.

Liu: To me, drama is an element of a good story. I can tell people that I had a meeting with John Kotter. But if I tell people, in the middle of the conversation, John Kotter stood up, left the sofa, and played on the piano just to illustrate something, it is more memorable.

Kotter: Correct.

Liu: That is drama.

Kotter: Correct.

Liu: And the story of Gerstner, that is drama.

Kotter: Correct. One of the concerns I have developed in the past, maybe for decades, is about the drama element. In a sense, the educational system of Harvard Business School was based on stories from the beginning, stories called "cases." I think it is because somebody back then intuitively said that this could be a good tool for education.

But if you look at the cases that were written in the 1930s, 40s, and 50s, they were different from the cases today. One of the most famous cases from the 1950s was still alive when I joined the faculty in 1972. It was two pages long, with no numbers. It was a story like, "Here's the situation. Fred does this. This is what happened next. So what should Fred do now?" Those sorts of cases don't exist anymore. The typical case today is thick, is full of numbers, and is boring.

Liu: Is that inevitable, given the nature of MBA education today?

Kotter: No. There is no reason a case can't be about a dramatic company, or dramatic problem, or solution to a problem.

Liu: But the beginning is always some catching scene.

Kotter: Should be. Or at least it greatly helps. Also, set the scene so readers can identify with the key person in the case, then go from there. That has not always been lost in how cases are written today, which is interesting.

Here is another way to see the problem. Who is a phenomenal storyteller? Steven Spielberg. Steven Spielberg will not be impressed by our cases. Even if he was trying to have people in DreamWorks—I don't know how many people are employed in the firm—even if he wanted them to learn more about management, I can't see him using our cases because he knows what a good story is and the power it can have.

Cases today are usually still stories. There are just less story-like than they were decades ago, which has to do with the development of analytical tools. And probably to some degree because economists have taken control of business schools.

Three Kinds of Leadership Story

Liu: I wrote an article a couple of years ago called "Learning Storytelling from Goizueta and Knight," about Robert Goizueta from Coca-Cola and Phil Knight from Nike. Actually, in Nike there was a storytelling program, telling stories about what Knight and Bowerman did in early times. That was emotional and touching. I was amazed. In that article, I quoted Noel Tichy, who said he got an idea from Howard Gardner that leaders should tell three kinds of stories. The first is "Who am I?" to identify a leader's values. The second is "Who are we?" to define the values of the leader's organization. And the third one is "Where are we going?"—which is the vision.

Kotter: I like that. I am not sure those are the only categories but, intuitively, I like it. With entrepreneurs who are very successful, it is the second of the three I see them keen to latch on to.

I was just on the phone with a well-known company that's been growing, but the entrepreneurial culture that helped make it so successful is beginning to die out, mostly because it has hired so many new people. One of the ways I have seen people deal with this problem is to come up with a good story, sometimes very much rooted in the earliest years of the company, that defines "Who we are." Then they tell the story in various ways. For new hires, new-employee orientation is an important part. Done well, that strategy can be powerful.

One last thing on stories. I have executives trying to turn companies around come to me on a regular basis. What I have learned over the years is before they give me the company background, its problems, all on PowerPoint slides, I say, "Just tell me, what is the story?" That is my leading line: What is the story. Often it shapes the conversation in a way that makes it a lot easier for me to understand what's going on, what their problems are, where they are trying to go, and how they had difficulty trying to get there.

It's also not unusual for people to come to me and say, "Our problem is communicating our vision. We tried this and that. Two levels down, they clearly don't understand." I say, "Fine. How are you communicating?" They hand me something, usually a thick pile of paper. I look through it. It is PowerPoint slide after PowerPoint slide: little dots, short sentences, jargon . . . and I can't figure out what they are talking about.

I find myself just spontaneously saying, "Have you ever tried wrapping this up as a story, and telling people at your meetings, and giving it to people to share the story with others?" In this case, it is more about the story of "Where we are trying to go." So, it is your third category. If put in 100 PowerPoint slides, some people will be able to understand because they are very analytical and they have just been through Harvard Business School. But most people haven't and won't get it. Even among the people who do get it, I am not sure how well they can retain that information. A good story about this fabulous future you and I are going to create together can stick more.

Different Personalities in a Change Process

Liu: If we go back to *Our Iceberg is Melting,* are you saying that it's just a new version of your old ideas?

Kotter: Well, yes and no. It is very much *Leading Change* and *The Heart of Change*. It throws in a few more little things that have to do with characters, and then offers everything in a very different package that is trying to leverage a good story, including the visual aspect. Putting in those drawings is not a random idea.

Liu: By characters, what do you mean?

Kotter: Nowhere in the other earlier books do we talk about people with specific abilities, personalities or the like, and how that affects change. The closest we come to is in the second step of leading change: when you create a guiding coalition, you want to get the right diversity of people to give you power to do something big. But it's pretty abstract. We decided to take it further in the iceberg book, to explore different personalities and how they contribute to a change process, and how they each can, in their own way, provide leadership at certain times.

A company in Dallas has turned this into a one-day training program with my permission. There is a big module that asks you to think about which of the characters in the book you are most like, and which of the characters are most like the others on the team you actually work with daily. It is a very interesting and useful exercise. That is what I mean when I say we have added a little bit more. I suspect there are a few more things in the book that I am not even aware of, or did not arrive at consciously.

Maintaining a Sense of Urgency

Liu: What else are you working on?

Kotter: My next book, which will be out in September,[2] is about urgency. In a highly successful large-scale change process, it is step one. I became convinced a few years ago that where people were most often getting stuck was literally in the beginning. They weren't getting enough of a sense of urgency among enough people, and that stopped them from getting any momentum, getting the right group together who were willing to spend the time and emotional energy on change, creating a good change vision, and so on. Not only did they not do it, they also didn't understand what they were missing.

So my new book is about urgency, and basically the argument is this: in an increasingly turbulent and fast-moving world, change is becoming more and more important. If you look at where people stumble, it's right at the beginning. So more people need to know how to create and maintain a moderately high sense of urgency. In this book, I spell out the tactics that people use or don't use.

Liu: What's the lesson?

Kotter: Well, the bottom line is, No. 1: the average urgency level of the typical organization out there now is too low. No. 2: the lack of urgency is increasingly creating problems. No. 3: there are specific tactics that people use to increase urgency. And No. 4: the tactics are not only mind-oriented but heart-oriented; they are not just analytical, but also emotional. A lot of this is about bringing the outside in, getting the external reality inside, which almost inevitably overcomes complacency.

It is not enough just to create urgency and go on to the next step; you have to both create and maintain it throughout the process. Even more important, as the world moves faster, organizations have change going on all over the place, all the time. In such a world, it is a huge strategic advantage to have a relatively high state of urgency almost built into the organization's DNA.

Combining Leadership and Management

Liu: In *A Force for Change,* you said not only is too much management and too little leadership bad, but too much leadership and too little management is also bad. You actually used China's Cultural Revolution to illustrate this.

Kotter: Correct.

Liu: I am thinking about Enron and WorldCom. Is that too much leadership with too little management?

Kotter: I don't know enough about the details in either one of those situations. But I do know an entrepreneurial situation where the key figure, basically the founder of the company, took an idea and created a new product, and the company took off. He was a good leader and really could get people to follow him. But because he didn't put in the systems and structures—the management stuff—the firm eventually went off a cliff. Without management to help stabilize and, to some degree, guard the leadership, it's risky. One of the biggest cliffs that anybody has run off in the twentieth century was the one you were just referring to.

Liu: But you were also saying that in this era we are short of leadership.

Kotter: Yes. A fundamental problem you find all the time is that the management is there in a firm, but the leadership process is not there, and that creates a particular set of predictable problems. The firm becomes too reactive. It has difficulty handling change, grappling with new opportunities, and ducking hazards. It is too stable, often becoming too internally focused, because management tends to deal with more of the inside than the outside. A lot of the smart companies today see the problem and are trying to deal with it by holding onto some intelligent management systems while starting to help more and more people to behave as leaders.

Aspects of Leadership Development

Liu: What is the most important thing for a company itself to do to train its potential leaders?

Kotter: There are many possibilities. The more that people at the top recognize that they simply have to develop the leadership potential, wherever the potential is, and keep developing it in themselves, the more they will find ways to do so. It can be inside HR programs or inviting outside speakers, but it is essential that it is incorporated into daily activities too. In the right sort of meetings, and with people telling good stories, you can create an environment that helps everybody take another little step toward becoming a better leader.

So leadership development becomes a continuous process, not an event. That's how you get leadership development.

Liu: So what you are saying is basically to keep a learning attitude, and put it into action to show people.

Kotter: And on a constant basis. Almost any setting, at any time, offers an opportunity for people to grow. If you can capitalize on those opportunities, people will start to grow.

An obvious place where you can help people grow their leadership potential is at yearly top management meetings. I make speeches in those settings all the time. It is amazing how often firms waste this opportunity, or send out messages that have nothing to do with good leadership. They set up a room with seats in a way where you end up with a lot of long, narrow rows that makes it look like a military command-and-control exercise. This is hardly appropriate for people who are as well educated as they are today, in an environment that is moving as fast as it is. We try to talk them into putting the chairs into a half-circle and do lots of subtle little things to encourage a new mindset.

Liu: There are different sayings about whether leadership can be taught or learned. I think most people, at least among leadership gurus, agree that leadership can be learned. What is your view?

Kotter: I have found that the best way to think of it is this way. Everybody is born with some leadership potential. For some of us, it is very small. For others, it is very big. So, potential is the first step.

The next step is developing that potential into skills. I have yet to find anybody that has developed all of his or her potential.

And the third step is actually using the skills in what you do each day. In my experience, this is very rarely done. People hold back for many reasons, including not having the courage to stick their necks out, or believing that leadership is the CEO's job, not theirs.

So the aim of leadership development is twofold. First, it is to develop potential into skills. Second, it is to get people to use those skills as often and as aggressively as possible.

Kotter's Leadership

Liu: Do you consider yourself a leader?

Kotter: I try to provide two kinds of leadership. One is thought leadership around the sorts of issues I write about. And the second, especially when I am in front of a crowd, is some actual leadership of groups and individuals. I try not just to give a speech to a crowd. I try to get people to, figuratively, stand up and start moving in a new direction because of the experience I put them through. So in that sense I am more a people leader, not just a thought leader. But I try to do a little bit of both.

Liu: What is your definition of leadership?

Kotter: Ultimately, leadership is mobilizing people to make great things happen. It is not about small things. I can get you to move your notebook four inches over there, but if I achieved that, nobody is going to say I just led you. Leadership tends to be about bigger problems and bigger issues, and about making great things happen.

It is also about mobilizing. People often do their thing, and slowly. Yet to make great things happen often takes a group effort, it takes energy, and it takes everybody marching toward a specific, sensible direction. And mobilizing is a good word, at least in English.

I like things short and simple. So, "mobilizing people to make challenging things happen." There you go.

Endnotes

1 In "The Power of Stories" (*Forbes*, December 6, 2004), Kotter wrote: "When Lou Gerstner became IBM's CEO, the company had become bureaucratic and inwardly focused. Early on, stories about Gerstner poured out of the executive suite, and everyone in the company realized in short order that things would be different. For example, at a first divisional meeting, where managers were accustomed to presenting great reams of overhead projections, Gerstner turned off the projector and insisted they all just talk. This story flew across the organization. Very quickly, having the best slides stopped being among the criteria for success at the company."

2 *A Sense of Urgency* was published by Harvard Business School Press in September 2008.

PART IV

Complexities in Leadership

CHAPTER 9

James March: Leadership and Life

James March is the Jack Steele Parker Professor Emeritus of International Management at Stanford University. Best known professionally for his writings on decision-making and organizations, he is a true polymath, being elected to the National Academy of Science, the American Academy of Arts and Sciences, the American Philosophical Society, the National Academy of Public Administration, and the National Academy of Education, as well as several overseas academies.

He established his reputation with two books written early in his career—*Organizations*, co-authored with Herbert Simon in 1958, and *A Behavioral Theory of Firms*, co-authored with Richard Cyert in 1963—which are considered classics in organizational studies. During his career he has been a professor of psychology, political science, management, sociology, and education. In addition, he has written eight books of poetry. Though primarily an academic, he was by no means an Ivory Tower recluse. Among his many outside activities, he established and chaired the Citigroup Behavioral Sciences Research Council and was a director of several companies.

While James March is not a household name among business executives, he is highly regarded by management gurus: in a "gurus' guru" list, published by the *Harvard Business Review* in December 2003, he emerged second, behind only Peter Drucker.

March admits that he gets more enjoyment from playing with ideas than selling them. It is said that he began his classes at Stanford each year by saying, "I am not now, nor have I ever been, relevant." He tries not to give advice on any practical matters. (In the course of our dialog, he joked that the only advice he gave to people is to "produce children.") However, that did not stop him from offering advice to his good friend John Reed, then CEO of Citicorp, not to proceed with Citicorp's merger with the Travelers Group.

March does not like to be called a guru or master. He sees himself as a teacher and taught Organizational Leadership from around 1980 right up until his retirement. This was highly popular among undergraduate and graduate students alike and was unusual in that its required reading included classical literature such as *War and Peace*.

March may have retired but his legendary teaching lives on in work based on his lecture notes for the course: a book entitled *On Leadership* (2005) and two films, *Passion and Discipline: Don Quixote's Lessons for Leadership* (2003) and *Heroes and History: The Lessons for Leadership from Tolstoy's War and Peace* (2008), both conceived, written, and narrated by March.

When I met him at his Stanford office in June 2008, the 80-year-old March was entertaining, incisive, and exceedingly enlightening.

How to Define Leadership

Liu: Reading *On Leadership*, it struck me that it is not usual to use literature—novels, plays, and poetry—to teach leadership.

March: The research literature on leadership is not very good. There are many assertions, many claims. Either it is hard to figure out what they mean, or there is not much evidence to support them.

In order to talk about leadership, we have to recognize the fundamental issues in leadership are no different from the fundamental issues in life. The fundamental issues in life are probably better discussed in great literature than they are in social science. So in my leadership course we would read some well-known books, including *Othello* by William Shakespeare, *Saint Joan* by George Bernard

Shaw, *War and Peace* by Leo Tolstoy, and *Don Quixote* by Miguel Cervantes.

Liu: How do you define leadership?

March: Well, I don't, because I don't use the term very often. What I think most people do is talk about people who sit at the top of some organization.

Liu: So you also refer to leaders as those people who have a top position?

March: Yes. Some people say leadership should be defined functionally in terms of people who get other people to do things or something like that. That's all right, but I don't think that is what most people mean by the word most of the time.

Liu: In your book you said, "There are two essential dimensions of leadership: plumbing and poetry." From this statement, I take it you don't distinguish leadership from management as some people do?

March: What I call "plumbing" is what most people call "management," and what I call "poetry" is what most people call "leadership." In almost any position in life, you need the mix, whether you're an artist, writer, manager, or plumber.

Plumbing and Poetry

In James March's view, leadership has two essential dimensions: "plumbing" and "poetry." The plumbing of leadership is the capacity to effectively apply known techniques, involving such everyday tasks as making sure the toilets work. It requires at least four components:

- *Competence.* People in organizations must know what they are doing to make organizations work well.

(continued)

(*continued*)

- *Initiative.* People will take initiatives to solve problems locally, promptly, and autonomously. This is accompanied by delegation and rules of tolerance.
- *Identification.* People in organizations have a sense of shared destiny, mutual trust, and collective identity, so they take pride in their work and in the organization.
- *Unobtrusive coordination.* The autonomous actions of individuals should be coordinated effectively, quickly, and inexpensively by such mechanisms as the prior specification of rules, the flow of signals and information, and the provision of duplicate (redundant) procedures as backup for critical activities.

March argues that these four things, conventional and standard as they look, are at the heart of effective leadership.

Apart from the mundane part of leadership, however, a leader should also be a poet who finds meaning in action and renders life attractive. For this purpose, a leader is equipped with power and words. Power is a means of encouraging other people to blossom, and with words a leader forges visions and evokes devotion.

How to Distinguish Leaders

Liu: Do you think great leaders share some common traits?

March: No. They share whatever traits we use to define them as great leaders. I think the evidence is very clear that in terms of personality or skills or intelligence or training, it is very hard to say there is anything to distinguish them consistently.

Liu: Some people say great leaders do some things in common.

March: Again, you can define the terms, so it is true. But I never found such an exercise very useful.

I told my students that there are several decisions you make very early in your life that will affect your chances of becoming a leader, and will have more impact than anything else we know about.

The first decision you make is who your parents are. The second decision you make is where and when you will be born. And the third decision you make is what your sex will be. Once you've made those decisions, you can account for as much variance as we can account for. Otherwise everything is a lot of idiosyncratic things.

Liu: So you're saying that the main factors known to influence whether one becomes a leader are outside of the individual's control?

March: That's right. We are not very good at predicting who's going to be a leader. There are a lot of studies trying to do that, but the results of the studies do not agree with one another. When I read them, I say: you can't tell.

How to Learn from *Don Quixote*

Liu: Let's talk about *Don Quixote*. You taught it in your leadership class, and made a film about it. I once wrote that you cited Quixote as an example of a great leader. Why do you think so?

March: No, I definitely did not say that. In fact I think you would have to say, looking at him, that he is not a good example of a leader.

Liu: But we can learn from him.

March: Yes. We can learn how to think about great actions.

In most of the Western world at least, the conventional justification for great action lies in the great consequences of the action. You act because you expect good things to happen as a result. That consequential logic runs through all our teaching, all our speeches, banners, posters, all the histories we write.

But for the most part, it is not true. Most people will discover that it's very difficult to accomplish great things. They cannot justify their lives in terms of the great consequences of their actions.

Quixote is important primarily because he reveals a second way of justifying great actions, which is really quite different. Quixote does not care about consequences. What he cares about is being a proper knight. In some way the most important sentence in that novel is "*yo sé quien soy*": I know who I am. Because he knows who he is, he does things.

He says, "What would a knight do in this situation? Then I'll do it." He is in love but for no other reason than that is what he has expected of a knight errant. So it's an attitude that says you don't justify great actions by expecting great things. You justify great actions because that is what is appropriate for the kind of person you are.

That is a vision that has its limitations, but it is a very important thing for great leaders.

Liu: The name of the movie is *Passion and Discipline*, so I think you are saying that great leaders should have these two elements.

March: That's right. Quixote has both. He is passionate in his commitment to his identity. He is very disciplined. He knows exactly what that identity requires. That's how he proceeds.

Liu: Just now you emphasized: "I know who I am." This is important for everybody, isn't it, not just for a leader? However, does Quixote really know who he is? He's not a knight. So shall we say that he does not know who he is, but he knows who he wants to be, or he should be?

March: This is a very shrewd observation. From many external realistic points of view, he does not know who he is. But he has a clear conception of who he imagines he is, or should be, or wants to be. And that is, I think, what our identities are.

Quixote has chosen a socially constructed identity. He didn't construct it. He just tries to live up to it. That's true of most of us. We have identities we try to live up to. They are not invented by us.

Liu: When you comment on Quixote, you say he substitutes a sense of identity for a sense of reality. Shall we also say that leaders should find a balance between a sense of identity and a sense of reality?

March: Yes, I would say so. My emphasis on Quixote is very much contextual. The people I talk to, almost all the time are totally committed to a consequentialist view of world, which says, I do things because of the consequences I expect to follow.

On one hand, it would be very bad to abandon that completely. On the other hand, I think they should have a balance between that and an identity-based conception. So in this culture, with these people, I push them as far as I can to Quixote. If they went all the way to Quixote, I would probably push them back the other way.

Thus, in other cultures, I could imagine taking a different position. I once wrote a paper called "The Technology of Foolishness." When I spoke about this once in a conference, one of the participants, who was from the former Yugoslavia, came to me and said, "Please, when you come to Yugoslavia, don't give this talk. We have enough foolishness." I think he may have been right. So it is a matter of balance.

Finding Joy and Beauty in Leadership

Liu: In your book you talk a lot about the joy of being a leader, which is unusual. People don't usually associate joy with leadership.

March: There are two things we don't talk about that are important. One is joy, and the other is beauty.

Joy is one of the most profound human emotions and expressions. I think we all want to seek that in our lives. It makes leadership too intensely serious to ignore joy, to ignore the properties of enjoyment in these activities.

I think it's OK for a leader to say "This is just wonderful!"— particularly if that joy is in the experience and not in the trappings, the crowns, the salaries, and so on, but in the intrinsic property of the job, the chance for creativity, and the opportunities for accomplishing things. I think nothing is worse than seeing a leader who is tired, who feels totally overcommitted, and has no sense of pleasure in what he is doing.

Liu: What about beauty?

March: I think one of our obligations is to make life a little more beautiful if we can, and particularly in the ordinary parts of our lives. I have a great deal of affection for people who manage to have little gardens to make their life better. And I have a good deal of affection for managers who can write memos that have some elegance of expression, who see these as pieces of poetry instead of just some documents.

Liu: Warren Buffett's name comes to mind here. His letters and reports to shareholders are wonderful.

March: They are often very wonderful. He's also one who gets joy out of his life, I think, without embarrassment about things like power and wealth. Yes, I think he is a good example.

Current Business Leaders

Liu: Who are the business leaders you admire?

March: I really don't know many of them. One who I do know and admire is John Reed. He is now retired, but he was, for many years, CEO of Citicorp. I think he is a good man.

Liu: Tell me the qualities you admire in him, and what other people can learn from him.

March: The qualities I admire about him are his analytical mind, and his willingness to do what he thinks is right. He has a considerable interest in research, so he thinks executives should be continually refreshing their knowledge. All of that I find useful.

When he negotiated the merger between Citicorp and Travelers, I told him I thought it was the craziest idea that he'd ever had, and it was dumb.

Liu: Why did you say that?

March: Because Citicorp was a company that had a certain kind of integrity and tried very hard to be a reasonable operation. And Travelers was a high-flying, finance-driven company.

Liu: A different culture.

March: A different culture, and a dangerous culture in some sense.

I liked his response to me. He said he appreciated my kind advice. You know, we were pretty good friends, so he was willing to listen to me, but he didn't change his mind.

When the merger did not go well and I reminded him of that conversation, he said he thought the merger was in fact good for the stockholders, but bad for the company.

Liu: Do you think it's a big problem that CEOs actually report to Wall Street?

March: I'm basically a retired researcher, so I don't know that I know enough. But I think certainly one of things that has happened over time is that the leadership of our business institutions has become more and more sensitive to Wall Street, and less and less sensitive to the businesses they are in. I think that's a bad thing.

Liu: I was surprised to read that you discussed current well-known business leaders like Bill Gates and Steve Jobs in your class.

March: As I said, my sense of them is entirely second-hand.

Liu: Your sense of Quixote is also second-hand.

March: Well, that's true. But I have no reason to think they're remarkably different from a lot of other people. We are inclined to imagine that history is made by a few spectacular great men. I don't believe that.

I have been impressed by Bill Gates's willingness to try to do good with his fortune through the foundation. I think he recognizes to some extent that this fortune does not belong to him. He senses that society has produced it. In that way I have a more positive feeling about him than I do about Jobs. But I am very reluctant to say anything about people I really don't know well.

Liu: You were talking about beauty. People will say that Steve Jobs is doing a beautiful job. He is making beautiful things. I don't know whether you agree.

March: Steve Jobs once left Apple and formed a company, NeXt, which did not do particularly well, and then managed to persuade Apple to buy NeXt and made more money. He has been given a lot of credit for creating an environment at Apple which stimulates innovation and a sense of style; those things I like. I like Apple's commitment to beauty in design. I think that's nice to have. I am not inclined to attribute all of that to Steve Jobs, but he certainly deserves some credit.

How Business Institutions can Stimulate Learning

Liu: In my experience, managers are not very good at learning. They don't know how to learn. Also they prefer not to learn, in many cases. That's my observation in China. I think that also happens in the States and elsewhere in the world.

So why does this happen? Why do people in organizations not know how to learn? Why do organizations sometimes not learn well?

March: We will start by recognizing that learning from experience in organizations is not an easy thing. The world they are trying to learn from is what I call a complex, noisy world with weak signals and small samples. Even the best minds will have difficulty learning in such a world.

There are some specific things we know which probably can help. The one that fascinates me is the extent to which we stop experimenting with new things too quickly. In a sense we learn too fast. We switch from an activity that is not doing well to another activity sooner than we probably should. In a world filled with noise and external distractions, an activity that appears to have poor outcomes might very well turn out better than we think.

Managers are often operating under considerable pressure to show results very fast. Learning requires experimentation and some longer time horizons. If top management gave a little longer time horizon to managers, and managers were a little slower to make inferences from small samples, they might get a little more useful learning from experience.

Liu: So you are advising companies to slow down, perhaps?

March: That's right. Did you hear about "slow food"? The fast-food thing has stimulated a counter movement of slow food, which requires you to take time.

How to be a Teacher/Leader

Liu: You are recognized in academia as a master. But you don't want to be called a master or guru. How do you define yourself?

March: I think of myself as a teacher. I try to be a teacher in a Quixote sense. I try to imagine what is appropriate for a teacher and I do that. A teacher feels happiness when students conceive our ideas and take possession of them, and see them as their own.

I have a granddaughter who was learning Hebrew, and she did well. When I congratulated her teacher on doing a very good job, she said, "I found a jewel, and I polished it." That's the way I feel about my students. They are jewels. My role is simply to polish them a little bit. After all, I will be forgotten, and they will be there.

Liu: Actually, in ancient Chinese language, learning has the same meaning as teaching.

March: In the Scandinavian languages, it's the same word.

Liu: I was wondering why you didn't call yourself a learner, but a teacher.

March: That is also very true. I've learned much in the world, most of it by teaching.

Liu: Many business thinkers advocate that business leaders should be teachers as well. What do you think about that?

March: I believe that. I don't like the word "mentor" because it suggests too much of a follower kind of relationship. Teachers try to create a setting in which the student learns. I think a manager should create a setting in which workers and other managers learn.

Managers should have a notion which is as hard for managers as for teachers to think: their victories are the victories of their students, not themselves.

Liu: Is it a teacher's job to give advice?

March: No, I don't think so. A teacher's job is to structure a world so that people see with their own eyes what they should do. I think I listen pretty well to my students, and intervene a little bit by suggesting "Have you thought about this? Have you thought about that?"

Liu: You are saying that a teacher's job is to create an environment in which students can reflect on themselves, and know how to learn. I still want to know more about how to create that environment.

March: I used to say that you have to drink wine for at least three years with someone before you can start to talk seriously with them. Don't start a conversation at the highest level. Relax, and create an environment in which people feel safe, in which they can express their feelings, and which is non-judgmental.

Then you can be very critical about particular writings, or particular statements. You say: "That's something you wrote and I am going to tell you that's garbage. That doesn't mean you are garbage." But in order to get that difference across, you have to establish a kind of a relationship that fundamentally says, "I am on your side."

Liu: And you just said you listen very well. I think that is a technique to set up relationships.

March: Absolutely.

Liu: You also have to ask questions.

March: Yes, often these are questions to which you don't know the answer. Much of the time, you are using questions to make speculations in which you don't necessarily believe.

My job is not to tell people what the right answers are, but to remind them that the answer they have at the moment is not the whole answer. So I am often saying different, perhaps contradictory, things to different people.

Liu: That might also be the leader's job—not to tell people the answer.

March: I could imagine myself in such a role and I am sure it would be very similar. The leaders I admire in those roles tend to be people who are not too ego-demanding. They are not too concerned about establishing their own position, or their own superiority, or whatever.

Liu: They are humble?

March: Yes, I guess. It's the Chinese philosophy.

Liu: I ask this question a lot. Do you think great leaders are humble?

March: Well, I think that's a tricky thing. They are and they aren't.

I grew up in Wisconsin, which is in the middle of this country. When you go from Wisconsin to the East Coast, you go from one kind of a culture to, in most respects, a higher culture. When someone from Wisconsin goes to New York, for example, they are humble, but they believe at the same time they are probably smarter than the people with whom they are dealing. So it's a genuine humility but combined with a genuine self-confidence—"I know I'm just a small pebble on the beach, but I'm a very tough pebble"—it's that kind of feeling.

Liu: How would you respond to being called a "thought leader?"

March: It's all right. I grew up in a family in which there are very smart siblings. One of the strongest of my father's values was that you do not claim to be somebody more important than anyone else. He beat it into us. So I believe that. That's the kind of society in which I want to live—where you would not claim priority. So I try not to.

How Context Matters

Liu: Your story of going from Wisconsin to New York reminded me of another question I had when I read your book. If we put it into a global context, you can say there are American, Chinese and European ways of doing things. Can we say there is a single right way? Aren't all these ways right in their context?

March: Absolutely. They fit into the context. All things are embedded in culture. When I went from Wisconsin to New York, again, one thing startled me. In Wisconsin if you are smart, you never say a word. But in New York, smart people are talking a lot. I made mistakes when I thought that guy was dumb because he talked a lot. He wasn't dumb. It's just different cultures.

Liu: So if we come back to our focus on leadership, we can say that there is no single leadership style that is right.

March: Absolutely.

Liu: It depends on the followers, the task, and the context.

March: Very much so. Of course, some leaders are multi-cultural or "multi-lingual." They can switch from style to style. That's useful. But I have known quite successful leaders who are very verbosely authoritative. I know others who hardly say a word.

It does depend on the context. Of course, you develop your own context.

How to Study Leadership

Liu: I am a student of leadership. What advice would you like to give to me?

March: I try not to give advice, but if you run a study of leadership, you have to recognize the term is not a very useful one. It is almost impossible to research since people have strong feelings about it. They can't hear you.

That said, I think leadership is a useful organizing term. But it's useful mostly to tell people: "Look, the way you are thinking about this is not the right way."

There are some phenomena associated with leadership. We know a fair amount about what happens when people are given formal positions of authority, and what they do, how that changes them. We know a little bit about how one participates in groups in order to lead people to reach a decision.

We may know some things about the problems in balancing personal life and public life. That's a big, important thing for leaders. And we know some things about tradeoffs between unity and diversity, between exploitation and exploration. Those are also useful to leadership.

So a lot of things are relevant to leadership, but don't explicitly talk about leadership, and that's the direction I would go.

I once wrote a little piece in which I pointed out one of the problems for leaders is they live in a world that demands clarity, clear goals, clear understanding and precise senses; but the world they live in is unclear and paradoxical, and so on. They know that. So they live in a world in which they have to speak one way and live another way. And that becomes intolerable for many people.

The point of that article is that leaders should read poetry, because much of the time poetry sees something through two lenses. Life is both confused and clear. Individuals are both admirable and despicable. Two things are going on simultaneously and you have to be able to see them both simultaneously, not in order to resolve the conflict but in order to see it as an essential element of life. I am not sure I've persuaded many leaders to read poetry as a result, but I think it might be good if I did. Or you did.

10

Joseph Badaracco Jr.: Leading Quietly and Morally

Joseph Badaracco Jr. is the John Shad Professor of Business Ethics at Harvard Business School and Senior Associate Dean and Chair of the MBA Program. His research focuses on business ethics, particularly on leadership and individual decision-making. He is the author of four books on these topics: *Business Ethics: Roles and Responsibilities* (1994); *Defining Moments: When Managers Must Choose between Right and Right* (1997); *Leading Quietly: An Unorthodox Guide to Doing the Right Thing* (2002); and *Questions of Character: Illuminating the Heart of Leadership Through Literature* (2006).

Leadership involves complex ethical issues without easy answers. In *Defining Moments,* Badaracco points out that there are two kinds of moral issues: the easy, which involve a choice between right and wrong; and the tough, which are the real test of leadership because the choice here is between right and right.

In *Leading Quietly,* Badaracco draws our attention to what he calls "quiet leadership." Quiet leaders are people who are not heroes in the organizational limelight and they don't act in a dramatic way. Rather, with modesty, restraint and tenacity, these leaders, usually middle managers, solve difficult problems with their careful, thoughtful, and practical efforts.

His most recent book, *Questions of Character,* is built on a "Moral Leadership" course he once taught. Its major reading materials—fiction and drama—are not typical MBA fare. Our conversation at his Harvard Business School office in October 2008, started from this unusual approach.

Works of Literature as Case Studies

Liu: You taught a course on leadership through literature. Why did you take that approach?

Badaracco: The basic reason is that we use case studies and these are descriptions of situations in which a manager has to make a decision. Works of literature are typically wonderful descriptions of situations in which somebody has made a number of decisions. So, fundamentally, they are like case studies.

The advantage of fiction is that, through the insights of the author, you really get a sense of who the main characters are, what they are thinking, how they are relating to each other, what they think about things they've done. So it's much more realistic and much more compelling for the reader than something written by me or you, or some other ordinary author. That makes these literary works great case studies.

In teaching courses on moral leadership, with works of literature you can look inside the person, you get a sense of their motives, and that's very hard to do with the typical case study. You might interview a CEO. He might tell you what his motives are. That might even be a best-faith effort to explain them. But there may be levels of complexity that the CEO doesn't reveal.

Liu: Professor James March taught a leadership course at Stanford for 15 years using the same approach. Do you know him?

Badaracco: I know who he is. But I have never met him.

Liu: When I asked him why he took that approach to teaching leadership, what he said was: "Fundamental issues of leadership are no different from fundamental issues of life. And when we talk about fundamental issues of life, the great literature is better than other leadership literature."

Badaracco: I agree. Part of this is that it engages the reader more and is more memorable. These books do offer a window on life. You know, case studies are also attempts to portray life. They are just not as well written.

Liu: I may be wrong, but I've noticed that you don't use literature from other cultures.

Badaracco: Very little. I used *Things Fall Apart* by the Nigerian author Chinua Achebe and, over the years, I may have used two or three others. If I do the course again—and I might do this in a couple of years—I'm going to confine myself to using two American books out of 15 classes. I'll really push myself.

Liu: Do you think literature is pretty much culture-specific? I'm trying to understand the difference in using literature from different cultures.

Badaracco: I think that there are important, maybe even profound, differences. When, for example, you are reading something in translation, these differences may not be apparent to you. The subtleties that will be obvious to a native speaker may well be lost in translation and, of course, you are looking at it from a different cultural perspective.

Defining Leadership

Liu: How do you define leadership?

Badaracco: I define a leader as somebody who is willing to take responsibility and who uses that responsibility to make a positive difference.

I'm not talking about great moments of history. It could be "quiet leadership." I'm not saying it's only in political life or someone who is known publicly. I think it's quite simple. Part of it has to do with character. That's why I emphasize taking responsibility. Part of it has to do with outcomes, which is why I emphasize making a positive difference.

Liu: I read somewhere that you defined leadership another way: "Leadership is a struggle by flawed human beings to make some important human values real and effective in the world as it is." This is very interesting. Could you elaborate on that?

Badaracco: That's a definition I use for moral leadership. That's a long definition. It does really reflect ideas that didn't find their way into the books and perhaps should have. Perhaps they'll find their way into the next book.

If you look at the characters in literature, they are flawed human beings and they do struggle. They're people with limitations and problems, not superheroes. The key word in "to make some human values" is "some." They have to choose. Literature often focuses, because it reflects life and engages readers, on dramatic moments of choice.

"To make some human values real and effective," that's what I mean by making a difference in my shorter definition. "In the world as it is" is the way of Machiavelli who is part of the literature we read. So it's not in the world that we hope to live in or might dream about. But in a world that actually is.

So in a way, the short definition I gave you just compresses and simplifies a lot of those elements.

Liu: Let's take an extreme example like Hitler. Does he fit into the short definition?

Badaracco: Well, I use the word "positive difference." Hitler was a leader. He was just an unethical leader, at least with respect to some of the terrible things he did.

Liu: So in your definition there's no bad leadership.

Badaracco: The longer definition says to make some human values, not all, but some important human values, real and effective. So that's a long version of the word "positive." By values, I don't mean anything that someone might value, like the extermination of another race. I mean some traditional set of values either in the Eastern or Western tradition: courage, virtue, compassion, things like that. So I think I rule out bad leaders. I want to rule out bad leaders.

Three Virtues of Quiet Leadership

Badaracco cautions that quiet leadership has to be looked at from the perspective of character rather than tactics. The character that sets quiet leaders apart consists of three unglamorous virtues: restraint, modesty, and tenacity.

- **Restraint:** Quiet leaders restrain themselves when they realize that taking a forceful stand on principle can make matters worse. Their restraint is active, vigilant, and often creative, since they use the restraint as a precondition for finding solutions to difficult problems.
- **Modesty:** Quiet leaders don't inflate the importance of their efforts or their likelihood of success. They are genuinely modest about the expertise they own and the role they play. They know there are many forces that shape what may or may not happen and many of the forces are beyond their control or influence.
- **Tenacity:** Quiet leaders have a sense of moral, emotional, and personal urgency, so they act tenaciously even when they have relatively little power. Tenacity matters as it runs counter to the virtues of restraint and modesty. Restraint and modesty are brakes without which a vehicle is dangerous, and tenacity is an accelerator without which a vehicle won't travel very far.

Quiet Leadership

Liu: Do you distinguish between leaders and managers? You define "quiet leaders" as managers who apply modesty, restraint, and tenacity to solve particularly difficult problems. Why don't we just call them quiet managers?

Badaracco: There's a conventional definition of leadership which tends to be associated with really important advances and great dramatic moments in history. I think that's just wrong. Those are moments of leadership, but it is a very narrow definition. It excludes too many other situations where something important happens but not in a dramatic, visible way. I think the central thing is the world being significantly different as a result of a leader's work, no matter how unheralded or unsung.

Liu: You mean it is the outcome that's important, regardless of whether this outcome is known by everybody.

Badaracco: That's right. If you think of it, it's only a tiny fraction of acts by leaders that can be widely known even within a society, or even within part of a country. So that's a very narrow definition. All I wanted to do in *Leading Quietly* was to sketch how people did not get a lot of publicity but still made a difference. Frankly, some of the techniques that are described are more associated with the standard definition of being a manager. I guess that's OK with me.

About 30 years ago, the political scientist James McGregor Burns made the distinction between transformational and transactional leaders. The transformational leaders change people's values, and everybody else is merely transactional. I think we need far more sophisticated ways of thinking about what he calls "transactional."

I'm trying to almost create a third case, or four categories. First, you have great leaders. Second, you have the crooks and criminals, people like Hitler. Third, you have the people who are mere managers who just have to work things out most of the time. But there is another category, where the problems are complex and not readily solved by exchanges and transactions. It takes elements of courage and some other qualities to make a difference. If you look at a lot of the great leaders in any society, most of the time they spend doing quiet leadership. They are doing something hard. They care about it. It takes courage and commitment. But it's not on television. So, if I have to divide roles, I'd say they should be divided four ways.

Liu: Where do whistleblowers fit into your scheme of things? As a result of their actions, problems may be solved but it doesn't always end up well for the whistleblowers themselves. They are often alienated by their colleagues, or they lose their job and are unable to find another. I feel that you may not approve of their behavior.

Badaracco: First of all, I'm inclined to put whistleblowers in the heroic category. They're taking big risks with their careers, their reputations, and their families. I think the quiet leaders are prudent people in general and they should take such actions as an absolute last resort. Leadership is about getting involved, taking some prudent risks, and trying to change things, as opposed to going out to a phone booth, calling the federal authorities, and sending in the men. So I do admire whistleblowers, but in the same way I admire heroic leaders: they do set important examples for us in courage, determination, and commitment to basic values. But I'm not sure they could be role models most of the time.

Liu: So heroic leadership is also desirable in your view, but you are just saying that people might neglect other types of leadership.

Badaracco: That's right. They might not pay attention to how to do it well. That's a problem if people only have in mind one typical type of leadership. Another problem is that they may have a situation that really calls for quiet leadership, but they have only one approach, the heroic one. They may try the heroic approach and make things worse. If you think the only opportunity for leadership is to be a hero, you may go on a moral vacation for a while, waiting for the great moment, when there are a lot of other things you can be doing quietly.

Liu: You have quoted Machiavelli in using the metaphor of the lion and the fox and advocating that successful leaders should be both.

Badaracco: Exactly. I think we have a bias toward the lions and against the foxes. But we shouldn't. We should have the right mix.

Ethically Sensitive Pragmatism

Liu: You once said that three interlocking elements in most leadership decisions are character, accountability, and pragmatism. I am curious about pragmatism. How do we distinguish between necessary pragmatism and unethical shortcuts?

Badaracco: First of all, in a good number of cases, there are some things that are intrinsically wrong. If they are intrinsically wrong, they are often legally wrong as well. So those are inappropriate, illegitimate shortcuts. Leaders shouldn't use them.

I think so much depends on specific situations. Some things, for example, may be unethical shortcuts with some groups but perfectly legitimate with others. Let's say, for example, you have two experienced investment bankers doing a financial deal. They are sophisticated players and I think it's legitimate for them to play certain games with each other: bargain, fake, bluff. But this would be inappropriate if one of the players in a similar transaction was relatively unsophisticated. You have to look at what the stakes are in any given situation. You have to look at people's motives. So I think a lot of the rest really depends on specifics.

Finally, if you stand within the boundaries defined by overtly legal and commonly accepted ethical behaviors, people differ. You may think I'm doing something that's a little slippery. I may think it's fine and I can explain myself to you. You may not agree. But I can actually give a positive account of why this was a reasonable and even appropriate thing to do. So I think this ability is the third thing I would emphasize: the ability to explain and positively defend something that may look to somebody else as a sleazy shortcut. It is a useful test.

Liu: You are a professor of business ethics. The reason I'm concerned about your advocating pragmatism is based on the reality in China. I think people in China have too much pragmatism right now. Did you hear about the tainted-milk scandal in China?

Badaracco: Yes.

Liu: It may be a minor affair here but it's big in China. People are very, very disappointed because big companies and business leaders previously regarded as ethical leaders were involved. People are very disappointed. I think that's just the tip of the iceberg.

Badaracco: The way I see pragmatism is never pragmatism by itself. It's pragmatism with accountability and character. Or, as an old professor here at Harvard Business School used to say, we are training here "ethically sensitive pragmatists." I think there has to be a tension built in. With pure pragmatism, you can have terrible problems. Even Machiavelli had pragmatism tempered or limited by the good of the state, the glory of the state, the independence and survival of the state. It wasn't merely the survival of the leader. Unless you have got some counterweight, you will have big problems with pragmatism.

Liu: Do you have any observations on different business ethics in practice in the East and in the West?

Badaracco: I'm not sure I can answer that because I'm not sure I can even answer the question about business ethics in the West. I have the impression from newspapers that various forms of minor corruption have been thriving and may have been more common in China than in the US. But no one should think such things don't happen here. In every society where you have capitalism, where you have opportunities, where you have human nature, and where you have some people who are smarter than others about social complexities, it will happen. So I'm not sure that there are profound differences.

Perhaps, if somebody studies it, they'll find that routine behaviors and expectations in China are different from those in America. One might look less ethical from the perspective of the other. I'm not sure one is necessarily less ethical. The Chinese may be simply playing one game and the Americans playing another. If you are playing one of the games and you know the rules, I'm not sure there's a big problem.

Liu: So ethics is rooted in culture. Something that's ethical here may not be ethical there.

Badaracco: We can carry that even further if we go back to the complicated financial transaction I mentioned earlier. Irrespective of the country, it really depends on the sophistication and power of the two parties involved. If they are roughly equal, it may be ethical; if they are unequal, then it's unethical. So much depends on the specifics.

Choosing Between Right and Right

Liu: You have said that an easy ethical issue involves a choice between right and wrong, and a difficult ethical issue requires a choice between right and right. Could you give an example that would require a leader to choose between right and right? How should the leader make that choice?

Badaracco: First of all, I think almost everybody knows the difference between right and wrong most of the time. Sometimes there are grey areas. Sometimes people are confused. Even crooks know the difference between right and wrong. That's why they try to hide it when they do something wrong.

Now if you are a manager, getting other people in the organization to do the right thing and not to do the wrong thing can be a real challenge.

But right versus right is even harder because you are pulled in different directions by things that are genuine responsibilities. These are situations where this is right and that is right and I can't do both of them. Or there may be three things like that.

It can happen when people feel an obligation to different parties or different ideals. Most people don't want to feel bad after they make decisions. They don't want to think they have let other people down, broken promises, or failed to meet some appropriate expectations. So they really struggle in those situations. The higher you get in the organization, the more likely you are to face such choices. The stakes get higher because your decisions make more difference to people.

Liu: When Chinese firms make tainted milk and sell it to consumers, they might think they are doing the right thing for shareholders or themselves. People don't do things they don't think right. They do things other people may think wrong but they themselves think right. Are they choosing between right and right?

Badaracco: This is what I meant when I said just now that people may very quickly become confused. If you put the question to shareholders: "Do you want to risk other people's health? Do you want to run the risk that your company will poison them? You will be implicated and you will bear all the repercussions." Shareholders will say no. If you say to the individuals: "Look, people will get hurt and you'll go to jail. Do you really want to do that? You really think that's right?" I think most of the time they'll stop.

There are people who are just sociopaths; they just don't care. So they would fit your description. They would say, "I think it's right. I heard them. I don't see anything wrong with it." And you say, "You are hurting other people. You are ruining the company." They say, "Well, there's always a risk and I have thought about it." There is something wrong with them psychologically. They just can't engage in the reality of the situation. And there are people like that.

Liu: I think after Enron business ethics courses are more popular in the US. Probably after this tainted-milk incident, they will be more popular in China. I hope so.

Badaracco: I expect so, at least for a little while. But for people to sustain an interest in responsible leadership they have to understand that in the long run, and often in the short run, responsibility leads to success. If you see the butcher put a thumb on the scale while weighing your meat, you probably won't go back to that butcher. In a world of networks and relationships, trust matters a lot.

Becoming Who You Are

Liu: When I read *Defining Moments*, I was very interested in your emphasis on becoming yourself. Why is becoming yourself important in leadership?

Badaracco: If people are working or leading in ways that they are excited about, that they are emotionally committed to, they are going to work harder and better, and they are going to attract other people to whatever they are working on. That's what I mean by becoming who you are. It's really doing something that's not simply a technical operation that you know how to do because you've had a lot of practice, but something you are really committed to because it's important in your life, because it is your life.

There are people in this country and, I suspect, in China as well, who start and lead firms not simply to make a lot of money, although they may like to make a lot of money, but because this is how they want to live. Often, these entrepreneurs launch a business, sell the business, make a lot of money, put the money in the bank, and six months or a year later, do it again. It's not about more money, because they have plenty. They even risk some of what they have. It's how they want to live. That's what I mean by becoming who you are rather than being a mere technician or technocrat or something.

Liu: Can you say more about the process of becoming who you are?

Badaracco: At any point in your life you know some things about who you are. There's often more to learn. And you learn that through experience—tough experiences or good experiences. You react to those experiences. You may get crushed. It may take you a couple of years to recover. You may become a much different person. So, we are not finished products.

Liu: Let us talk about reflection—something you emphasized in your book. How does reflection help us to know more about ourselves?

Badaracco: A lot depends what you are reflecting on. If you take the time to look back, for example, you may see things about yourself, traits, skills, things you haven't noticed before. I think that's really hard to do. You often need somebody else to say, "You know you think you are this, but you are also like that too." Sometimes you can look back and say, "Well, you know, that is true. I just behave that way." So you can get a kind of self-knowledge.

There's also reflection in the middle of a situation, looking forward to some decision you have to make, to something you have to do. The reflection is more on what you care about, what your values are, what kind of person you are, and to some extent maybe what kind of a person you want to become. That's different from looking back simply to understand yourself. It's looking forward with the hope of shaping yourself, behaving in a certain way, living in accordance with certain values, and making certain commitments. I think these are the two basic kinds of reflection that are really quite different: looking back and looking forward.

Liu: What's your recommendation for business leaders?

Badaracco: At the end of *Defining Moments,* I wrote a little bit about Marcus Aurelius, the Roman emperor and Stoic philosopher. He took time to reflect. I think leaders typically need to. It's really hard, if not impossible. First of all, they are people who like action. Secondly, they usually have full schedules.

Liu: I don't know whether you know this but Marcus Aurelius's *Meditations* is selling very well right now in China, the simple reason being that the Chinese Premier told people that he read that book every night.

Badaracco: That's fascinating. The book has been around for more than 1,800 years; so it must be good.

American, Japanese, Chinese

Liu: Many people are saying of the Chinese version of *Leading Quietly* that the idea of quiet leadership is very Chinese. Were you inspired by some Chinese thinkers?

Badaracco: As part of the preparation for the book, I read a book by Professor Tu Weiming, a Chinese professor at Harvard, on Confucius's *Chung Yung,* or *Doctrine of the Mean.* One of the early drafts of the book started with a quote from Professor Tu.

Liu: So you were influenced by Chinese philosophy.

Badaracco: Yes.

Liu: I know you also taught in Japan.

Badaracco: I have been to Japan many times. When I discuss this there, people often say this is like a Japanese approach.

Liu: You have been to Japan and observed leaders there. What's the major difference you have found between Japanese business leaders and their American counterparts?

Badaracco: I don't want to exaggerate the difference because I think there are some fundamental similarities. There are some basic ways in which human nature is the same. Human nature aside, there is also the fact that business problems bring people closer together. Someone has certain technology, somebody else wants a license, and they have to come up with a contract with certain specifications and certain theories of payments. So we are not talking about Western or Eastern culture. We are talking about a deal. That tends to bring people closer together.

Another similarity is what you would call modern management. Accounting, finance, organizational structure, these things are quite common in many parts of the world. They may be used differently, interpreted differently, but there's often a lot of similar technology. I don't just mean in the narrow sense of chips or manufacturing technology. There are a lot of things that close the gap.

Liu: I agree. But there is always a gap. What is it?

Badaracco: My sense is that in Japan, there's much more patience and sensitivity to the nuances of situations and to people's individual thoughts and feelings. Americans tend to go ahead more directly, sometimes confrontationally and roughly, just to get things done.

Liu: Are you saying that Japanese people are more emotionally intelligent?

Badaracco: Very good American managers do have a high degree of emotional intelligence, but not always. I am inclined to say yes.

Liu: Any other differences?

Badaracco: I do think what's said about Japanese management is true. They spend a great deal of time preparing to make a decision, discussing options to a decision, looking at the implications of the decision, and so forth. So when it's time to make a decision, everyone is pretty much on board.

Liu: They build consensus.

Badaracco: Precisely. I think consensus is just valued more heavily. Also, even though I said that modern management brings people closer together, when Americans think about business and success, they tend to be thinking about short- to medium-term profits. I don't think that is the case traditionally in Japan.

Liu: Do you have any particular impressions of Chinese managers?

Badaracco: It's only an impression. I wouldn't want to get into trouble. But my sense is they have some similarities and styled behaviors to Japanese managers, but I think they also have some similarities to American managers: the focus on returns and a willingness to be direct and aggressive more often than their Japanese counterparts.

Being direct and aggressive is something of a last resort in Japan. It's the starting point often for Americans. For Chinese, in my impression, it is one tool among many, but they are ready to use it.

CHAPTER 11

Manfred Kets de Vries: Leadership on the Couch

Manfred Kets de Vries, a Clinical Professor of Leadership Development, holds the Raoul de Vitry d'Avaucourt Chair of Leadership Development at INSEAD, where he is also the Director of the Global Leadership Center and program director of management seminars on leadership and change. The author, co-author, or editor of more than 30 books and 300 scientific papers, he was the first non-American recipient of the International Leadership Association's International Leadership Award for "his contributions to the classroom and the board room" and the Lifetime Achievement Award for his contributions to leadership research and development. He has also been elected a Fellow of the Academy of Management.

A practicing psychoanalyst and management scholar, Manfred Kets de Vries has been "putting leaders on the couch," both literally and figuratively, for many years. Trained in economics (University of Amsterdam), management (Harvard Business School), and psychoanalysis (Canadian Psychoanalytic Society and the International Psychoanalytic Association), he brings a fresh view to the study of organizations and is particularly known for his clinical approach to leadership. By going inside the mind of leaders, he discloses how their earlier experiences have shaped their behaviors and vulnerabilities, and makes recommendations for healthy leadership and organizations. The *Harvard Business Review* has commented of him that "that no other leadership scholar had as much exposure to the mind of the business leader."

By telephone from his INSEAD office in October 2009, Kets de Vries talked to me about his "clinical approach" to leadership, the darker side of leadership and possible ways of dealing with it, and other prescriptions for effective leadership in a post-heroic era.

A Clinical Approach to Leadership

Liu: As a leadership scholar, you are characterized by what you call a "clinical approach" or "clinical orientation." What is the clinical approach to leadership?

Kets de Vries: The clinical approach is basically an abbreviation of two major themes. One is psychodynamic. The recent financial meltdown in the West is a good indication that people are not really rational decision-makers—lots of other things are at work that should be taken into consideration in the decision-making process.

The other theme is systemic, meaning that you have to see things in context. You have to view people in the context of their family, their culture, and their work environment. Organizations also need to be looked at in this way. A systemic view gives you a more realistic perspective in dealing with knotty situations. So the clinical approach refers to the psychodynamic systemic orientation to looking at people in organizations.

The clinical approach deals with the fact that the main part of our behavior is not truly rational. Like it or not, much of our behavior is outside conscious awareness—a factor that some people find hard to take. To have an inkling of what is going on outside of conscious awareness, we need to pay attention to emotions. Nothing is more central to who we are than the way we express and regulate emotions.

In addition, we have many defensive mechanisms—some are quite primitive, others very sophisticated. We all have a shadow side. We have a tendency to avoid troubling aspects of our experiences. There are many distressing thoughts and feelings we are reluctant to deal with.

Furthermore, we are a product of our past—many things that we learned in childhood will determine the way we behave in adulthood. The past is the lens through which we can understand the present and shape the future. Scratch an adult, and you find a child. So if you want to understand a person, you have to get a better sense of the context where he or she comes from. I have discovered that everyone is normal until you get to know them better!

I began to study these behavior patterns particularly when I looked at toxic organizations with dysfunctional organizational environments. I became interested in how leaders can create "neurotic" organizational cultures. In one of my earliest books, *The Neurotic Organization*, I tried to establish an interrelationship between personality, leadership style, corporate culture, and patterns of decision-making.

It is interesting to note that the world has been dominated by economists. I used to be an economist myself and always felt that the rational economic model didn't work. It has been shown recently in a fairly dramatic way—the financial meltdown—that this model is not realistic. Economists, from being more econometrically oriented, are now suddenly all becoming behavioral economists. Making such a turnaround is probably not enough, but at least it is a step in the right direction. They have begun to realize that there are many other factors that they need to insert into their economic models.

Liu: Why did you take a detour from economics and embark on this less-traveled road?

Kets de Vries: I started as an economist, but I went to Harvard where I studied management, and became interested in psychoanalysis. I became a management professor at INSEAD and Harvard. Later on I became a psychoanalyst. So I have tried to integrate three disciplines: one is management, with a particular focus on strategy and organizational behavior; another is economics, particularly business economics; and the third is psychoanalysis in its widest sense, and with that come family-systems theory, cognition, neuropsychiatry, evolutionary psychology, and so on. Many different schools of psychology, fortunately, are converging.

Basically I am a pragmatist; I want to do things that work. That's my philosophy. I want to create organizations that are good places to work. Making that happen has been a major motivator for me. I am trying to create what I have called "authentizotic" organizations, places to work where people feel alive—because many organizations where people operate are like gulags. They are not very nice places to be.

Liu: What does "authentizotic" mean?

Kets de Vries: The first part comes from the Greek word *authentee-kos*, which means "authentic." I use authentizotic to describe an organization where leaders walk the talk and reveal the meaning in each person's task. The second part comes from another Greek word, *zoteekos*, which means "vital to life." In authentizotic organizations, people are invigorated by their work and feel a sense of balance and completeness, a sense of effectiveness and competency, a sense of autonomy, initiative, belonging, and creativity. The prime challenge to organizational leadership in this new century is to create corporations with these authentizotic qualities.

Liu: You have said that your main objective in studying leadership is to "bring the person back into the organization." What do you mean by that specifically?

Kets de Vries: When I started to study organizational behavior the focus was on structures and systems and how to make them work. Instead, I have always paid particular attention to the role of people in the organization. For example, I run two major year-long programs at my school. One is a CEO program for top executives. I created this program with the fantasy that if I could influence the minds of those 20 people in my seminar, who are probably responsible for a few hundred thousand people, it might affect their organizations in a positive way.

Another year-long seminar is called "Consulting and Coaching for Change." In this seminar I try to help HR directors, people in consulting and coaching firms, and line managers to become better at people management.

I am interested in programs that help people change for the better. Most leadership programs are actually only Band-Aids; they don't do very much. You know, after people go through that kind of program they get a temporary high: they feel good, particularly if they have had good teachers, and then, unfortunately, they go back to normal. I want to create programs that have a true impact, that help people change, that push people to take important steps in their personal and organizational lives. As a result, at INSEAD we have developed the second-largest coaching center in the world, the Global Leadership Center. Apparently, our clients find the work we do very useful. We also have the largest center in group coaching, because I think group leadership coaching is a very effective way to help people change, given the pressures participants put on each other.

Understanding the Inner Theater

Liu: You emphasize the importance of understanding one's inner theater. What is the inner theater, and why is it so important in a leadership context?

Kets de Vries: The inner theater relates to questions like: What are the things that motivate you? What are the things that are important to you? What are you deeply passionate about? How do you feel about certain things? How well do you understand how you affect other people? All these things have to do with a person's inner theater. I help people to understand themselves better. If you don't know what you are doing, it is really hard to be effective in many ways.

If you want to be an effective leader, it is important that you have a sense of what you are all about; what you do well, and are not so good at. If you are not good at certain things, maybe there is something you can do about it, or maybe a better strategy is to find people who can complement you. We live in the age of what is sometimes called the "post-heroic leadership" era. We all may be looking for a messiah to save us, but that's not going to work.

We will be disappointed. Barack Obama, for example: the world is now looking to him to make something happen. He has to manage expectations very carefully, otherwise there will be a backlash. Real change is driven by teams of people.

Of course, when we get anxious, we all wait for somebody to help us. It is like when we were children and looked to our father or mother to get us out of difficult situations. But in the modern organization—with highly complex, matrix-like structures and very diverse, virtual teams—the trick is how to have the different parts working together, how to work in teams, how to build good lateral relationships, and how to trust each other. That's important. In my workshops, I do a lot of interventions for top executive teams about exactly these things, because most are not functioning very well.

Liu: What are the specific things you do to help people understand their inner theater?

Kets de Vries: As a start, I have developed many questionnaires. For example we use the "Global Executive Leadership Inventory," which is a 12-dimension, multi-party, leadership feedback instrument, giving you some sense of how you are perceived as a leader in your organization. Then there is the "Leadership Archetype Question-naire," another multi-party feedback instrument that helps executives identify their specific leadership style, and helps them to create effective teams. I also use a "Personality Audit," which gives you feedback about how people who know you very well (family members and friends, for example) perceive you. Another instrument is the "Internal Theater Inventory," and I am also introducing an "Organizational Culture Audit."

So I use lots of instruments that jump-start the process of understanding your inner theater. Helped with the information from these instruments, you can have courageous conversations with the people you work with, something that doesn't usually happen. The insights provided by these instruments help people see what they usually do not see—and find ways to do something about it. Remember, when one person tells you that you have ears like a donkey, ignore it. But if two people tell you, get yourself a saddle.

Liu: I read your new book, *Sex, Money, Happiness, and Death,* and my impression was that you were saying that all human decisions and most management decisions are driven by sexuality.

Kets de Vries: No, that's not what I'm trying to say. Sexual desire is important but not the only driver. In that book, I try to make the point that we have different motivational need systems: some are physiological and of sexual-sensual nature; some are of an affiliate/attachment nature, originating in the mother-child relationship; some are exploratory, creating the base for creativity and innovation; and some are aggressive, associated with the territorial imperative.

Many decisions, however, have a strong sexual component. When I wrote that book, I had to contemplate this seriously and read evolutionary psychology closely. When you look at Paleolithic man and contemporary man, where we come from, and how the sexes interrelate, you get the sense that there is a strong argument to make about the continuation of the species, and sexuality of course plays an important role in this.

In my work, I listen to stories that people tell me about their lives, and beyond all the superficial things to do with organizational issues, or whatever—below the surface—you find many other concerns. Some of these have to do with sexuality; some with death or fear of death; some with happiness, or what makes us happy; and some with money, which of course stands for many other things, like power, influence, and so on. At the time I wrote the book, I was involved in three other books on leadership, organization, and coaching, and I wanted to write something very different, to do with meaning. That was why I started the project.

It also grew from my irritation about the outlook of many business schools, which can be extremely narrow and are often directed by professors who don't have much of a systemic point of view. Many business schools have forgotten what makes up their clientele. They sit in their ivory towers doing their own thing, totally detached from the reality of life. Basically, I am in the business of helping people. I think in many business schools there is a sense of detachment, of having lost sight of their clientele, a preoccupation with writing some very abstract things that have nothing to do with the people they deal with—which brings us back to my wish to "bring the person back into the organization."

Liu: So sexuality is one of the major actors in our inner theater?

Kets de Vries: It is one of the more important ones. No question about it. I am not saying anything original when I say this. I have many predecessors who said so, Freud being a very important one.

Of course we don't say these things out loud; it is a no-no in organizational life. It is hard to say: "Listen, I really like your secretary. I really desire her." So we find all different kinds of ways around such thoughts. We try to sublimate them. We try to avoid having women in certain decision-making bodies because their presence would stimulate such thoughts. But certainly it's there and many decisions depend on it. People do not necessarily confess to this unless you enter into deep conversations: "Why did you decide to make a trip abroad to meet somebody? What is the real reason behind the decision? What's going on there?" It is like a subterranean world.

To get a better understanding of these things, an important thing I try to teach my students is to use yourself as an instrument, stand apart from what people say and think, "What are they really saying? What is really behind the statements? What do I feel listening to this person?" In other words, how to really listen with the "third ear," as it is called.

The Darker Side of Leadership

Liu: You stressed the darker side, or the shadow of leadership. Could you elaborate on this here?

Kets de Vries: Actually, I first became well known as the pathologist of organizations, meaning that people came to me when things had got really bad. In management now we find the emergence of positive psychology and positive organizational behavior. This is fine, but we have to be realistic. Total optimism can only get you so far. We all have a darker side. We have seen the terrible things people do to each other in times of war and on other occasions.

Frequently, this darker side is induced by past experiences. To quote the philosopher Soren Kierkegaard, "Life can only be understood backward; but it must be lived forward."

I think one has to deal with the past; we have to see things in perspective, otherwise we will not learn anything. What was effective when we were young, may no longer be effective when we are adults. We need to obtain that insight to be able to change.

I was asked by the *Wall Street Journal* the other day about the financial sector, and I said that I got the sense they have learned nothing, and seem to have forgotten everything. After the financial meltdown these financial engineers caused, they seem to have reverted to normal. Their feeling of entitlement is back. Once again, they are "masters of the universe," giving themselves all these outrageous bonuses. Obviously, it is easy to come to terms with the dark side.

Yet talking only about the dark side is not good for morale. Take my own career: after many years studying the darker side of leaders and organizations, and being a leader in that field, I founded our leadership center at INSEAD, became its director, and began to look at the other side of the equation—What can I do to make things better? So, I've shifted a bit, but I've never lost sight of the darker side. You know, you need to see things in perspective. It is dangerous to become like the positive psychology group and emphasize that everything is OK—that's not the way things are. It is not being realistic.

Liu: By the darker side of leadership, I think you mainly pointed to executive failures and said that "transference lies at the heart of the mystery of executive failure." Could you explain why?

Kets de Vries: Transference can be described as a false connection. It refers to inappropriate repetitions of relationships that were important in our past, but are acted out in the present. These unconscious, repetitive tendencies of interacting with others in a certain way affect not only the way we love, choose friends, or express ourselves, but also influence patterns of relationships with bosses, colleagues, and subordinates. Transference reactions also affect the way we make decisions, our leadership style, many other aspects of our work, and non-work related parts of our lives.

Being in a position of authority may increase transference reactions. For example, the moment you are in a leadership position people start to project their fantasies onto you. Unfortunately, the recipients of these projections may start to believe them. It is a very insidious process. If this continues, people who are the outlets of these transference reactions may become totally full of themselves, and lose their capacity for reality testing. The moment you are in a position of authority, people have a tendency to tell you what you want to hear. That has been the failure of too many leaders. I see it over and over again in organizations: leaders start to believe their own press and lose touch with reality. You don't learn much from people who always agree with you. Prime examples of such dark leaders are Hitler and Stalin. In the case of Hitler, people didn't want to say anything against him, so reality was lost and the organization, in this case Germany, went down the drain.

People should always have a healthy disrespect for their boss. Of course in certain cultures it is more difficult. For example, in Malaysia, given existing power differences, it is more difficult for people to be able to create give-and-take situations than in countries such as Sweden or Finland. So, cultural factors also play an important role.

But many of the CEOs I've met have told me that when they are in a position of power, people push them into becoming more and more narcissistic. Lord Acton's statement, "Power corrupts, and absolute power corrupts absolutely" contains a grain of truth. A dose of narcissism is needed to attain a leadership position, but soon the combination of disposition and position can produce a narcissistic disorder. Many of the executives I meet don't know how to deal with this kind of emotional contagion.

Get an Organizational Fool

Liu: One of the solutions you've proposed to this problem is having an "organizational fool," as in the fool of William Shakespeare's famous play *King Lear*. You've said that every leader needs one.

Kets de Vries: Yes, but it's a more idealistic than realistic statement, because fools don't usually make it to the end of the play. But it would be good to have an inner circle of people, or sometimes a network of people, who serve as a realistic sounding board, who are able to tell top executives how things really are. For example, in my CEO seminar the participants form a strong network. They can really serve as a mirror to each other.

That is why leadership coaching has become so popular: it's one way of testing reality—at least when coaches are not too hungry for money. As a matter of fact, many CEOs have nobody to talk to. So if the coach isn't too hungry, he or she can tell the CEO, "Listen, I don't think this is realistic. Maybe you could do things differently." One of my most effective coaches, a former CEO of a large company, has a lot of business experience and people do listen to him. He has no specific agenda and isn't out for money, so he is not a hungry consultant and can be very frank with senior executives.

I have a number of relationships with Russian CEOs, some of them larger-than-life, very powerful people, who are likely to shoot people who tell them, "You're full of shit. It doesn't make sense to me." To have a realistic sounding board—which coaches can be—should be a deliberate act on the part of the CEO and other senior executives.

Liu: It is a beautiful idea to have the organizational fool, but it seems to me very hard to put it in a concrete form in current organizations. As you said, it is idealistic.

Kets de Vries: It's not easy to be an organizational fool. I've seen a few organizations where they have one, but it's not a long-term proposition. But when I think of the fool, I think of the French "*morosophe*," the wise fool. You can find someone who is in a senior position in the organization, and has no ambitions to take the place of the top executive, and is independent enough to give courageous feedback. I do a lot of work with global consulting firms, and in some I play that role by being fairly frank in giving feedback. Having courageous conversations is the only way you can add value. Generally, we learn from people who disagree with us. Wise executives should make that a rule.

Who are the Potential Leaders?

Liu: You don't agree that everyone has leadership potential. Who, then, are the people who are more likely to become leaders?

Kets de Vries: Since I am in the leadership development business, I cannot say, "You're either born a leader or not. And that's it." That's not acceptable. I strongly believe that you can accentuate a person's leadership potential. Some people, however, do have a head start.

A person's leadership potential is a delicate interplay between nature and nurture. If you grow up in a family where your parents very much encourage you, push you to do something with your life, and maybe give you some solid values about doing something for the world, it's more likely that you'll turn into a leader than if you come from a very dysfunctional family. But then again, some people who have had a very difficult upbringing have become highly effective leaders.

I have seen examples of both. For example, I wrote a number of case studies about Richard Branson, the founder and owner of the Virgin conglomerate. Looking at his family background, we see two parents who loved their son, were very supportive, and encouraged him in his various entrepreneurial ventures. But I've also seen situations where people come from very miserable circumstances, having experienced many hardships—deaths in the family, separation, divorce, and so on—but have never been hopeless. They felt they could make a difference. They would say, "I'll give it a try. I'm going to show these people and the world that I can do certain things." So there are many different combinations and variations on this theme.

Becoming successful is dependent on the very complex interface between leaders, followers, and the context they operate in. To be the managing director of McKinsey requires a very different leadership style than if you are running a steel mill—many factors play a role.

An effective leader is a little like a Zen riddle, or *kōan*—a paradox: a leader has to be active and reflective, an introvert and an extrovert. A leader has to be engaged in divergent thinking, and in convergent thinking. A leader needs IQ as well as EQ. A leader has to think atomistically as well as holistically. A leader's thinking has to be both short-term and long-term. The person who can balance these contradictions effectively will do well.

Liu: How do you define leadership?

Kets de Vries: Leaders get extraordinary things out of ordinary people. As the saying goes, people will work for money but die for a cause. The key question is, how to get that extra effort out of people. Of course, leaders need to provide focus. They need a good understanding of what makes their people tick. They have to walk the talk; they need to set an example, otherwise they are not believable. Leaders need to be good at execution. After all, a vision without action is a hallucination. The defining factor, however, between mediocre and great leadership is always the same: the creation of meaning. I genuinely believe that the most highly effective leaders are the ones who are good story-tellers; they know how to tell the stories that provide meaning in their organizations. Maybe this isn't so easy if you work for a cigarette company, or a company that makes weapons. But when it comes down to it, people are searching for meaning. I hear it all the time.

Incidentally, I have worked with the World Economic Forum, and the fellows and directors there are an extreme example of people looking for meaning: they want to change the world for the better; they want to leave a better world for their children. I think that is a very laudable idea. It is a great motivator.

Beware of Charismatic Leadership

Liu: Some business thinkers, such as Peter Drucker and Jim Collins, have argued that charisma is more of a burden than an asset to a leader. We have also seen in the real world that a lot of business and political leaders perceived as being charismatic have turned out to be poor leaders. What is your view about charismatic leaders?

Kets de Vries: Charisma can be used for the good and the bad. Obama, for example, is a very charismatic leader. We'll see how he turns out in due course. But many charismatic leaders have been very costly for society. Hitler was a good example of a charismatic leader who used his position for the bad.

I'd like to point out again that we live in an era of post-heroic leadership, meaning that the "great man" theory of leadership—it's usually a man, by the way—is a very dangerous thing. The best organizations are highly team-oriented and concerned about charismatic leaders. Ideally, there should be safety devices around leaders: unfortunately, with political leaders, things can become very difficult. Robert Mugabe in Zimbabwe is a good example. He is a very charismatic leader, but he has lost touch with reality; he has become addicted to power. He wants power at any price, and damn the people.

Actually, as we are talking about charismatic leadership, it's interesting to remember that paranoia is the disease of kings. Some time ago I wrote a book on Shaka Zulu, a famous, nineteenth-century Southern African king, someone who changed the geography of Southern Africa. His paranoia was of the worst kind: he lived for about 40 years and during his reign left about two million people dead. So be aware of charismatic leadership, and the paranoia and the human suffering that come with it.

Charismatic leaders are nice people to talk and write about, of course. I have written about many, including one of the most famous charismatic leaders of all times, Alexander the Great. Alexander conquered the world in 11 years, but after his death his whole empire fell apart. As a matter of fact, the acid test of a leader's success is how well his or her successor does.

Everyone who has reached a leadership position has the potential to assume charisma, because people project their fantasies onto them, as I mentioned when we were discussing transference. Transference and charisma are closely linked.

Liu: How is this different from the claim that not everyone has leadership potential?

Kets de Vries: Do you want to be a leader? To some people, that's a key question. We all have leadership potential if we want to pursue it, but, as I said, some people have a head start because of their background. Often, it is important to have a number of significant leadership experiences early in life—being class president, for example. Having a leadership position in the army, for many people, can be a defining learning experience. Think about some of the people fighting in Afghanistan now. Certainly it's a real challenge; you have to deal with life-and-death decisions. So that's the first thing that comes to mind.

As I mentioned earlier, when you are in a leadership position, like it or not, people will project their fantasies on you, and it's up to you how you deal with that, for good or bad. For example, I am the leader of the leadership center here at INSEAD, and quite a few people work for me. I have to manage their fantasies. I have to try to create an atmosphere of give and take. I want people to speak their mind. I want people to object when I say something that they disagree with. I guess I've been relatively successful in doing so because recently we did the cultural audit and my center seems to do quite well by comparison with other parts of the school. So I try to practice what I preach. I want to deflate the fantasy part, and want them to see me as I really am. That is also the role of the leader. Leaders have to manage people's fantasies carefully; otherwise, they may lose touch with reality.

Prescriptions for Effective Leadership

Liu: In your book *The Leadership Mystique*, you summarized four "Hs" for effective leadership: hope, humanity, humility, and humor. If I asked you to summarize the essentials of effective leadership now, would you still use those four Hs or something else?

Kets de Vries: It's easy to remember acronyms. Of course, real life is more complex. But if you are asking me to summarize the essence of leadership, I would still start with hope. Leaders are merchants of hope; they have to speak to the collective imagination of their people to create a group identity. Hope is really another way of saying leaders have to provide focus, vision, or whatever. You have to help people to have focus to manage their existential anxieties.

The second thing is that leaders should have integrity, meaning that people should trust them. An organization that has no trust in its leadership will not do well in the long run. If you say we need to go through a downsizing exercise while, at the same time, you give yourself a raise, you will not be believable. If you say that people development is important, but you don't develop your own people, you aren't believable. So you have to walk the talk. Integrity is important. If people don't trust you, forget it.

The third thing probably has to do with courage, being decisive. Leaders need to have the ability to make tough decisions, and also to make decisions in crisis situations, not sit on their hands.

Another element has to do with emotional intelligence. People are different, which is what I try to teach the participants in my programs. People have different inner theaters and different motivators. Some people are entrepreneurial, so you just tell them, "Do your own thing." Some people are very dependent, and you spell out what you need from them. Others are counter-dependent, so you say, "Listen, I don't think we can do it," and they might do it just to prove you wrong. So you have to figure out the important factors that motivate people; you have to be very good at emotional sense-making. Some of those things are, of course, mixed up in the four Hs idea.

Of course nobody is perfect, but some have more talent to take on a leadership position than others. If you don't have all the qualities needed for the environment you are operating in, find people who can complement you. I have seen leaders who are terrible at certain things, but they know they are terrible, and find others to help them. Self-awareness is critical.

Liu: Is there anything in particular you would like to add about the financial meltdown?

Kets de Vries: At the moment, in the West, we are living in a very difficult time. Because of the financial crisis, many companies are deeply involved in cost-cutting. But cost-cutting gets you only so far. Eventually, you are cutting into the muscle and bone of an organization. We should not forget that the real money in business comes from innovation, from creativity, and from doing new things. It is not easy to be really creative when cost-cutting is the only creative idea. It is hard to do new things while being subjected to a gulag-like atmosphere. It is hard to be a "survivor."

For creativity, for playfulness, leaders need to create a culture where people can have fun. I mean enjoying yourself, feeling pleasure, and being playful. Creativity and children's play are very closely related. When there is a playful atmosphere in the organization, there will be a greater likelihood that new things will happen.

Balancing EQ and IQ

Liu: You emphasize emotional intelligence a lot, so I would like to talk a bit about it. Is emotional intelligence something people are born with?

Kets de Vries: No, I think that is wrong. From a biological point of view, emotional intelligence is probably more spontaneous in women, because of the physical relationship between mother and child. Mothers (in most instances, much more than fathers) have to interpret signals from a non-verbal person, the baby, who cannot yet talk. Mothers usually spend more time with the baby, which is partly induced by their hormonal structure. So in that respect, when you ask whether people are born with EQ, you may be right to suggest that we are predisposed toward it.

But many elements of emotional intelligence can be learned or developed. That's what I try to do with the people in my CEO seminar. I am impressed when I compare the way they make interventions in the first week of the program, to the way they perform a year later, in the last week. At that point, they are much more sensitive and they make much better interpretations, so there definitely is a learning curve.

Liu: You also said that "acquiring emotional intelligence and becoming a Zen master are learning processes that have many aspects in common." So it seems to me that you can learn to acquire emotional intelligence, but that it is a long, long process.

Kets de Vries: It takes time; any form of change is not an instant process. I am not a believer in short programs. There are no quick fixes. There are no miracle cures: "Come to me for three days, and you will become emotionally intelligent and a charismatic leader"— that's bullshit. Americans have a tendency to make these claims, along with their fascination with self-help books. Developing yourself, and understanding yourself, is a journey. Like becoming a Zen master, it takes time. It is not something you can do by reading a book.

Liu: In many cases, becoming a Zen master can take decades.

Kets de Vries: To become a psychoanalyst, which I am, you have something like 10 years of training or longer before you graduate. But it doesn't mean you can't expedite things and help people to acquire emotional intelligence. Like Zen practice, it's about learning from the interface with your teachers: you listen to the comments made by the Zen master and try to understand what he is trying to tell you.

Liu: People pay more and more attention to EQ now. Isn't IQ also important in leadership?

Kets de Vries: Sure. Let's face it: it is important to have the ability to understand complex issues. However, too much IQ isn't always a good thing. You may intellectualize or rationalize things too much. Again, it's a question of balance. If you have too much IQ, you may be paralyzed; you can't make decisions anymore, because you're always thinking about other options. For example, when I think about the people I work with, many of them directors of premier strategic consulting firms, these people are very smart; they have a very high IQ. But I wonder sometimes if many of them really can become effective CEOs. When put in real situations, they may see too many options and may become paralyzed.

Liu: I have talked to another psychologist, Robert Sternberg, about leadership. He argues that contextual intelligence is very important.

Kets de Vries: He's right. One thing we try to teach people at our school is the contextual intelligence of the culture. For example, we now do programs in the Middle East, and my leadership coaches are struggling with the context, because they don't understand it very well; they don't always pick up on subtle signals. So they are learning, but given their exposure to many other cultures, they're probably picking it up more quickly than the typical Midwestern American would.

Leadership in the World

Liu: There are many "leadership gurus" in the United States, but very few in Europe. Why is that?

Kets de Vries: I don't know. But I read a list of "the world's top 50 management thinkers" recently and discovered that I am on it—so there is some hope for Europe. To be more serious, in the first place, I think management as a discipline has very much been a product of the US. If you look at developments in the East—China, India— many of the American paradigms are being questioned and over-ruled. At the moment, though, management theory is still dominated by American business schools. For example, when you look at our faculty (who come from all over the world), most have done their doctorate in America even though their first degree might have been from China, India, or elsewhere.

It is interesting to speculate about the influence Southeast Asian management will have in the future. What might be the effect of Islamic management, for instance? I have no crystal ball to see what is going to happen.

Liu: You have seen a lot of CEOs from all over the world. Do you think there is an American leadership style and a European leadership style? A Japanese and a Chinese leadership style?

Kets de Vries: There is probably a distinct Chinese and Japanese leadership style, but it is difficult to talk about a European leadership style, because Europe is really a very complex entity with so many different countries. The famous Globe study divided the world into various cultural clusters. For example, in Europe, you have the Scandinavian way of decision-making, the Germanic way, the Italian, Spanish, Portuguese, and Russian ways, are all which are quite different. We aren't talking about minor differences here. It is difficult to talk about a "European style."

I've hoped sometimes that there would be more convergence, but it's not easy. I doubt if my generation will see it. Perhaps the generation after me will. With increasing amounts of travel, and exchanges of people, there is going to be an increasing amount of convergence. As far as Europe is concerned, alone we can do very little. Together, we can do a lot. In this context, I have always liked the quote by Benjamin Franklin, one of the founding fathers of the US, who once said, "We must, indeed, all hang together or, most assuredly, we shall all hang separately."

PART V

Eastern Perspectives on Leadership

CHAPTER **12**

Cho-yun Hsu: Leading the Confucian Way

Cho-yun Hsu is the University Professor Emeritus of History and Sociology at the University of Pittsburgh. Before he began his teaching career there in 1970, he was Chairman of the Department of History at the National Taiwan University. One of the most distinguished Chinese historians in the academic world, he is the author of more than 40 books and 100 articles in Chinese and English, including *Ancient China in Transition: An Analysis of Social Mobility, 722–222 B.C.* (1965), *The Han Agriculture: The Formation of Early Chinese Agrarian Economy, 206 B.C.–A.D. 220* (1982), and *History of the Western Chou Civilization* (co-author, 1988).

Cho-yun Hsu has various audiences. As a professor of history teaching widely in the United States, mainland China, Taiwan, and Hong Kong, he has the traditional Ivory Tower audience. As a commentator on current affairs, particularly those in Taiwan, he is one of the leading liberal intellectuals to a much wider audience. Now, partly thanks to the burgeoning economic developments in China, he has been attracting a third audience: those keen to learn leadership and management from an historical perspective.

He was the recipient of the 2004 Award for Distinguished Contributions to Asian Studies, the highest honor from the Association for Asian Studies, in recognition of his "life-long dedication to the advancement of Asian Studies in the international arena," including his academic work which "revolutionized the field of Chinese agrarian history." In a speech at the Library of Congress on "Traditional Chinese Wisdom and the Business World," he proposed that entrepreneurs today could learn from Chinese history on how to promote business success.

He speaks to business people and to history students with the same enthusiasm. A series of his collected lectures in book form—on leadership, on management and on organizations from the perspective of Chinese history—provokes new thoughts on leadership and management. I spoke to the renowned 79-year-old historian at his residence near Nanjing University, during his visit there in October 2009.

Leadership through an Historical Lens

Liu: As a distinguished historian, you are known in the academic world for having "revolutionized the field of Chinese agrarian history." But you also have an audience, especially in China, who know you as a speaker or writer on management and leadership from a historical perspective. How are these two things connected?

Hsu: My study on management and leadership was derived from my own historical observations. I especially emphasize Chinese history because in Chinese history there's 2,000 years of bureaucracy. I regard two features in Chinese bureaucracy as deserving of our attention as references for our discussion of modern organizations. One is a meticulous procedure to recruit capable persons by means of open contest, and a system to check the performance of incumbent officials. Another feature was a relatively independent body of the "censorial board" to serve the role of watchdog and whistleblower. We may revisit these issues later in our discussion.

Bureaucracy, whose purpose was managing the empire, itself was a complex of organizations. It had two sides: the institutional side, which consisted of the government; and the personal side, which consisted of the actors on the stage, including the emperor himself, the source of power, and his helpers—prime ministers, ministers, and so on. The entire bureaucracy was set up to help the emperor, who exercised personal authority over the whole structure.

Therefore I see both leadership and management visualized and reflected in the Chinese history of bureaucracy. That's the reason I cut into this particular area called management and leadership.

History to me is a huge database. We usually derive experience and general principles of learning, especially about management and leadership, from the cases of existing corporations. Yet the history of incorporated firms is no more than 200 years old, while we have 2,000 years of data there, laid aside without being touched. Why don't we just use that bigger, more complicated database with a more visible track of revolutions or changes? That will help us to understand better these phenomena of leadership and organization.

Liu: So is leadership one side, and organization or management the other side, of the same coin?

Hsu: To me organization is the institutional side, and leadership is the personnel side. Leadership is the control of personnel. Organization is the institutionalized structure in which to place all those individuals, the slots for a particular set of people. But each set of people has its own personalities, cultural background, and behavioral patterns. No two sets are alike. Hence we have to face both, the structural, functional side, as well as the personal, individual side.

Therefore what I regard as leadership would involve cultural elements, psychological elements, personalities, and so on. On the organizational side we see the economic, sociological, and political elements. They reflect the two sides of the same question but they're not really totally separable. They are mutually supplemented and interactive parts. You cannot envision leadership without structure or vice versa.

Leaders should have a Sense of History

Liu: David McCullough, an American historian who specializes in American presidents, thinks it is very important for a leader to have a sense of history. Do you agree with him?

Hsu: Sure, even the history of the American presidency itself is little more than 200 years old. The United States is a man-made corporate body with a Constitution as the source of its governing authority. Every president has certain roles and functions defined by the Constitution, yet each faces a totally different scenario and a set of different problems, which are not static, but dynamic. Without history you cannot understand the backdrop to a certain scenario. Without this, you cannot understand why George Washington and Thomas Jefferson behaved so differently from Abraham Lincoln, and Lincoln behaved so differently from Franklin Roosevelt, and why Barack Obama and George W. Bush are different.

That's the very reason that history is a necessary tool for studying the American presidency because the presidency is a public role and its public setting is constantly changing and evolving.

Liu: You are saying that we should understand history to understand public leaders. But should leaders themselves understand the history to perform better?

Hsu: Sure, and for the same reason. It holds true for business leaders too. A business leader, say the CEO of General Motors or Bank of America, also must take note that he himself is located in the middle of the American scenario of his time. Each of these organizations has a history going back almost 100 years; they have their own histories, legacies, traditions, burdens of the past, and current issues which they must deal with, and they need to foresee what may happen tomorrow or next year.

Therefore even business leaders need to understand a broader sense of history—the history of the corporation itself, the history of the time at which it began, what it has become, and what it is going to be.

Liu: Harvard Business School has conducted a study on great American business leaders in the twentieth century, a major finding of which is that their success depended tremendously on contextual intelligence. And from what you said, the historical context should be a major contextual aspect.

Hsu: Yes, and a very complicated part. These contextual situations involve not only the public history or the corporate history, but also the particular actors' own life history.

Obama's Sense of History

Liu: The current US president might be said to have a sense of history. In January 2008, when asked which book he would take with him to the White House if elected, Obama, singled out *Team of Rivals*. It's a book about Abraham Lincoln's leadership during the Civil War authored by another historian, Doris Kearns Goodwin.

Hsu: You've hit a very important point. Obama projects himself as another Lincoln. Lincoln completed the first step toward Civil Rights by engaging in the Civil War and liberating the slaves. Being an African-American himself, Obama envisions his mission as completing the work started by Lincoln, which means bringing everybody into security, equal privilege, and equal duty. He purposely shapes himself as a successor to Abraham Lincoln.

But don't forget that he also implicitly envisions himself as being the successor of the legacy of Franklin Roosevelt's New Deal. Roosevelt started the New Deal, which remolded the economic system called free-market capitalism, injected into it a good deal of the workings of the welfare state, and adopted a dose of socialism to cure the problem of capitalism at the time. The so-called free-market economy, in fact, does not exist. All markets are somehow controlled, depending on who controls it.

Liu: And to what extent they control it.

Hsu: That's right. Now, in the middle of the current economic crisis, Obama and his generation envision that we are facing another crisis of free-market economy or capitalism, and this is more serious than the previous one. Hence, he vowed that he would dedicate his time to make health insurance and social security better. This has become his mission, for which the people gave him a mandate.

So he has his sense of his place in history, as a successor to Lincoln and Roosevelt. He wants to complete their unfinished work. Frankly, such a job never can be finished. It's always an ongoing one.

Mao Tse-Tung's Sense of History

Liu: I was wondering whether a sense of history falls into two kinds: one is healthy and helpful, and the other is unhealthy and destructive. For example, Mao Tse-tung had a great sense of history but did terrible things.

Hsu: Mao Tse-tung mastered tactics and control, to overcome others, to win people over to fulfill his personal ambition, but I doubt he ever had a sense of the value of humanity, or the sense of the meaning of human life. He might not even have understood Karl Marx. The young Marx was full of compassion.

Mao's primary target was power. He was thirsty for power and determined to achieve his goal. He had no inhibitions, so he could be ruthless, even brutal and cruel. He was prepared to do anything to win.

Lincoln was different. He sincerely believed in his Christian faith and he sincerely believed that God creates human beings as equals. Jefferson, too, had a vision. In principle, this was that we should lay down firm ground for good governance so that all individuals have the freedom to enjoy their endowed human nature, to enjoy beauty, to practice in their life what they choose, and to pursue goodness.

The difference between Jefferson and Mao is as wide as two ends of any spectrum can allow.

Tactics vs. Vision

Liu: So actually you are saying that a sense of purpose is more important than a sense of history.

Hsu: That's right. However, if you have purpose only, you can be bookish or a big dreamer and not able to achieve your goals. In the real world you have to deal with all kinds of irrational problems, and you have to deal with so many different walks of life. You need some skills to be able to handle people, but that should not be an excuse for you to forget or betray cherished human values.

Liu: Yes, but I don't think "a sense of history" just means learning tactics from history.

Hsu: You can do both.

Liu: Research on business executives shows that the further back you look, the further ahead you can see.

Hsu: There are two things. One is vision. One is lesson. You studied at Harvard, and you know Harvard Business School is well known for its case studies of corporations that succeed or fail. But here is the problem: more often than not, they study the successes. But, to me, the best lesson is learning from failure.

Allow me to say one thing. Success is the summation of many rational and irrational elements. You take only one chance to be successful, but you take a thousand chances to fail. While success is more rare and idiosyncratic, failure is common and more likely to follow a pattern. So if we study leadership in history, we better study failures. They give us a lot of better lessons than studying successes.

Zizhi Tongjian ("Comprehensive Mirror in Aid for Government") is a history book from the Song Dynasty through which the writer Sima Guang and his colleagues tried to tell current leaders how past emperors and ministers succeeded or failed. The most important phrase in the book is "Guang remarks"—the author's own comments. We see more "Guang remarks" on the cases of failure than on the successes. So to me studying history is a way we learn from other people's blunders, failures and fumbles, and try to avoid them.

However, if you only learn tactics, you only see day-to-day life. You do not see in which direction you are going. Hence, vision is important. You foresee what will happen, what may happen in the next 10 or 20 years, and prepare for that eventuality. Brokers on the stock market only prepare for the next hour, CEOs of big firms prepare for the next five years, and great corporate leaders project 10 or 20 years.

Liu: Do you see a lot of great corporate leaders?

Hsu: Unfortunately, no. Nowadays, shareholders' stocks are so much more fragmented that nobody can take from a general shareholder meeting a real meaningful discussion. CEOs don't need to report to their shareholders. Hence the CEO only needs to concern himself with his own annual report; he can then jump from this boat to another to double his salary or get a big bonus which comes from fabricated earnings. This kind of uncontrollable CEO is the basic problem of the current crisis.

Liu: How far ahead should great business leaders be able to see? Why do you choose to say 10 or 20 years?

Hsu: The best leader should be able to see at least one generation into the future. A big corporation like General Motors should be able to look one-quarter of a century into the future. Unfortunately, they didn't do that.

Why did we get stuck with the current gas-running car? Because the automobile industry has spent its capital, time, and energy to make the market stable for so long; it didn't want things to change. With good vision they would have been able to see that this source of petrochemical energy is being exhausted, that the global environment is getting bad, and that we'd better be prepared for change. But so far, not a single leader has done that.

The Call for Intellectual Leadership

Liu: As you have observed, CEOs face huge pressures from competitors, Wall Street analysts, stockholders, and so on. So to what extent can they play their role as a leader?

Hsu: There are many kinds of public leaders, political leaders, corporate leaders, and intellectual leaders working and interacting together. They sometimes reinforce one another, sometimes cancel one another out. Foreseeing ongoing change should be the job of intellectual leaders, because political and corporate leaders are busy with how to keep the government running, or how to make the best profit. Looking into the future is not really their full responsibility. Public leaders should assume the task, but they are not trained to do it.

Intellectual leaders should do it. Unfortunately, in the United States we haven't had great philosophers for almost a century. To me, the really great intellectual leader is Karl Jaspers, a German who was somewhat isolated even when he was alive and even today his voice is not listened to. My colleagues at universities in the United States all work on fragmented little issues. There is no voice shouting "Pave the road, and prepare for a new era." Nobody's doing that.

Liu: What is Karl Jaspers' main message we should pay attention to?

Hsu: In his book *The Origin and Goal of History* (1953), Jaspers noted that in each of the great cultures, a cultural breakdown had led to a great breakthrough that ushered in what he refers to as the "Axial Age" (that is, the age in which transcendental values were initiated as crucial premises of these cultures). He predicted that there would be a breakthrough into the era of scientific-technological culture within the next century. His insight is meaningful today. The crisis we are facing currently is indeed the writing on the wall that the modern world, which started at the time of Enlightenment, is facing a cultural breakdown.

However, without intellectual leaders to point out the future direction, there is a poverty of vision. Fortunately, in Europe, we are beginning to see public movements, such as the environmentalists, standing up. It's only because of their pressure that global warming and carbon consumption have become issues of great urgency. Public pressure forces public leaders to make decisions and the business leaders follow.

In the United States, in the past quarter-century, Shmuel N. Eisenstadt, political scientist and sociologist, and about 20 other persons, including me, have met 10 or 15 times in different locations in an attempt to point out to the world what we have learned from the past and what the future should be. Though these are heavyweights in the academic world—I am the lightest of them—the general public is not listening.

Liu: Is it like the Club of Rome?

Hsu: We don't have a name. We meet; we disperse. We try to teach our students, try to speak at public lectures, try to write books, and try to influence. But you know, the American general public does not read. Corporate leaders do not read. George Bush and his men did not read either.

Liu: But Obama reads.

Hsu: Yes, Obama reads.

Chinese Books for Leaders

Liu: If you had the chance to recommend a Chinese book to Obama and other world leaders, which one would you pick?

Hsu: The *Analects*.

Liu: In your writings, though, you always mention *Han Feizi*.

Hsu: That's right. Han Fei, the author of *Han Feizi*, predated Machiavelli by 1,700 years. Han Fei's time was the Warring States Period on the eve of unification, resembling what we have today. *Han Feizi* made the most sophisticated discussion on how to organize bureaucracy, and that is exactly what we are facing now. He tried to persuade leaders to organize a rational machinery for governing the world, instead of governance by individual groups, regardless of whether they were aristocrats, warriors, or rich people.

Today we are on the eve of globalization. We are actually passing through the last part of the Warring States. We need to prepare for another way. So that book should be very interesting and timely. Our problem is that in the days of globalization, we nevertheless still stick to the Renaissance concept of the sovereign state. The world is correlated, and we should make sure it has no boundaries. So far, a real united world remains a dream. For us to reach that point would take a long, long time. Yet, in the Warring States Period, to reach a unification of China was a long, long dream too.

Liu: So you think *Han Feizi* is very timely given the current global context. Then why do you recommend the *Analects* instead?

Hsu: Because in the *Analects* the main theme is the discussion of human values. Confucius and his students spoke of the principle of interaction between individuals: "Don't impose on others what you don't want others to impose on you." This Golden Rule is about tolerance and coexistence.

Liu: The Confucian Golden Rule is different from its Christian counterpart: "Do unto others as you would have them do unto you."

Hsu: It is good that you take other people's positions and want them to do whatever you like, but that means that you may impose your way upon others. That is precisely the American problem. The Americans have been leading the world for such a long time, but nobody has thanked them for it. Their attitude is "My way is the better way. You follow me." The Chinese believe in not doing unto others what you don't want others to do unto you. This prevents you from imposing yourself; it's for toleration.

So these two Golden Rules, the Christian and the Confucian, are very different: with a single positive, you are imposing. With double negatives, you are yielding and tolerating.

The central theme of the Analects is *Ren*—humanness. What are you? You are human. You are endowed with the born nature of humanness in your mind, in your structure, and in your being. All these are integrated into a whole piece. You are endowed with human nature as *Ren*.

Ren is a combination of *Zhong*—faithfully doing what you should do, and *Shu*—letting others do their part, giving them leeway, giving them space and freedom to do whatever. These are high and noble notions. Yet in reality we have problems because in human nature there is another part, which is selfishness. The Song Dynasty was the only dynasty in Chinese history really governed by Confucian scholars. With a fair process set up, they had an almost free hand to do whatever they liked; the emperor seldom interfered. The result was nearly a disaster.

The Song Dynasty history was full of factional struggles because everybody believed that he was thinking the right way. Hence, it happened that well-intentioned people fought each other. The result was chaos. They cancelled out each other's efforts, nullified each other's good work, and wasted energy and goodwill. Eventually, foreign enemies marched in. So this case of failure makes us think.

Liu: It is also interesting that it was in the Song Dynasty that the famous saying: "One can lead a country with half a volume of the *Analects*" began.

Hsu: That was an anecdote attributed to Zhao Pu, the first prime minister of that dynasty and a bureaucrat, rather than a well-educated scholar. The *Analects* is a collection of many short statements, and you cannot separate this part from that. What he meant was, if you put only a small portion of ideas of the *Analects* into practice, you can unify one country in peace.

Liu: Can we say, then, that the *Analects* is the guiding principle and *Han Feizi* is the tactics?

Hsu: Yes, exactly.

Developing Leaders in the Confucian Way

Liu: Let me get to another big question. As a historian, you have studied a lot of leaders in history. What are the great leadership qualities?

Hsu: I single out three things: vision, courage, and knowledge. To acquire knowledge is the easiest part, especially today—you may always have a good team of advisors and helpers. Courage takes personality. Vision takes wisdom. Not everybody can have the same vision. It's endowed; it's God-given.

Now, look at Obama's government. I am very pleased to see that he chose Steve Zhu as Secretary of Energy, because the energy crisis is upon us, and Steve Zhu has vision. But his economic advisors, all of them trained as econometrists, believe in numbers and money theory. Frankly, today's problem is not a money problem; it is, rather, a culture problem. And these economists are technocrats; they do not see broad visions. So Obama is riding a *troika*, three horses heading in three different directions. How to put them together? He has problems.

Liu: The bestselling book *Leadership Challenge* identified four qualities of the best leaders, which are forward-looking, honest, competent, and inspiring. I think competent here equates with knowledge, and forward-looking is what you mean by vision. What do you think about the other qualities honest and inspiring?

Hsu: Today many politicians lie, and many CEOs cheat. They are not honest. So honesty is a cultural problem. This is what we need most. We should remedy it soon.

Liu: By cultural problem, you don't mean Chinese culture or American culture?

Hsu: No. I mean the general human culture.

Liu: How about inspiring?

Hsu: That is a skill and also a kind of talent. For instance, Franklin Roosevelt, Abraham Lincoln, and Winston Churchill were good orators. They could use language to persuade and convince others. Ronald Reagan, too, had a reputation for being persuasive but I really don't feel he deserved this. But he was a great communicator. He could convince people, even by misleading them.

This is a talent. Obama has it, but he is not as strong as Lincoln, Roosevelt, or Churchill. Bush could never do it.

But such talents can be learned. Public schools in England, like Eton and Harrow, train people to talk, and then they keep using the oratorical art in parliamentary debates. They are good speakers. The election system of the United States does not train people in the real art of convincing people. Some ghost writers can write a good speech. However, this is not a spontaneous reflection of the thought of the real speaker. And in mainland China, the leaders are confined in such a small circle that they don't need to convince people. More and more we'll see people deliver speeches on television, less and less on the street, so the art and skill of inspiring people is not easily available now in leadership.

Liu: You are touching on another big topic: how can we train a leader?

Hsu: In the Confucian tradition, it starts with nurturing good habits in daily life: "*Sasao, Yingdui, Jintui.*" *Sasao* (sprinkle and sweep) is real action, *Yingdui* (reply and answer) is conversation by discourse, *Jintui* (advance and recede) is proper manners. The Confucian tradition would train people with these mundane, yet fundamental, behaviors. Also, Confucius said that learning includes language and ethics. Why does language stand alone? It is a good skill to make people know what you think. Most people today don't have real training in such a skill. In history, people of good cultural background did receive such nurturing; however, I am afraid that few such nurturing processes are available today. In Confucian ideas, it takes a combination of good manners, solid knowledge, and logical argument to constitute proper rhetoric.

Leaders Need Truth from a Friend or a Jester

Liu: We were talking about leadership qualities. What do you think of being reflective or introspective? Is that important?

Hsu: It is important. A person needs to take a step back to see what he did yesterday and what he did right or wrong. He needs always to reflect. But he cannot do this alone. You need good people to tell you whether you are doing right or you are doing wrong. That's why, in Chinese history, the relationship between Emperor Taizong of the Tang Dynasty and his loyal advisor Wei Zheng became such an oft-quoted episode as a leader who was willing to listen, and a subordinate who was not afraid to speak the truth. In reality, though, their interactions were not that coherent. Emperor Taizong was not so willing to listen all the time.

While this tale might be a myth, like George Washington's cherry tree tale it is useful. You do need people to tell you what you are doing right or wrong. A good leader should have somebody to tell the truth, and it would be better if he is a friend, rather than a subordinate, helper, or assistant. Franklin Roosevelt had a friend, Colonel Howe, who talked to him every evening. I don't think Mao Tse-tung had such a friend.

But it is not necessarily a friend. It could be a strange role, like in Shakespeare' works, where court jesters often played the role of telling the truth to their masters.

Liu: We had that in Chinese history too. Emperor Wu of the Han Dynasty had Dongfang Shuo.

Hsu: That's right. But in Shakespeare, you see so many of them. In *King Lear*, for example, the jester has the freedom to speak, and it is often the jester who reveals the truth, the cruel truth.

Liu: But it's not institutionalized.

Hsu: In ancient Chinese history, we had the institutionalized *Jian Guan*, the imperial censor, whose responsibility was to tell the emperor "you are wrong" and who could never be punished for doing so. But historically, there were very few such loyal critics. However, the logic behind such an institution is laudable, indeed.

Liu: And in corporations we don't have that.

Hsu: We have what is called the whistleblower, but this is not a built-in corporate institution.

Liu: And usually whistleblowers don't end up well.

Hsu: In America today, shareholders have become fragmented, so there are no real general shareholder meetings anymore. No more general meetings, so no more real board. No more real board, so the CEO has a free hand.

The Enron case was the big signal—we never really realized that. The Enron case was exposed because of whistleblowers. Theoretically we do have built-in whistleblowers: auditing. But auditing has no teeth.

Liu: And auditing can be bought, as the Enron case also showed.

Hsu: That's right. So government supervision is necessary now. But the American and British law is: if no crime is committed, we don't barge in and prevent it; we can't assume people are criminals. Hence nobody supervises American corporations.

Obama has the idea that the government should exercise certain supervision over business and markets. That is the major reason that the Republicans say he is a communist. The Republicans never realize that in the modern economy the hand never was invisible. The invisible hand is money in the hands of the wealthy. They can manipulate it. You and I cannot.

The Accidental Teacher to Business Executives

Liu: When and how did you start to teach leadership and management with an historical approach to business executives?

Hsu: It was all by accident. In the 1970s when the Taiwan economy gradually took off, one former student of mine married into an entrepreneur's family. She told them: "My teacher often told us a lot of lessons from history. Can't we learn from him?" So they invited me to give a talk to the department heads and general managers of their family business. They raised questions and I answered them. Gradually it became a routine lecture series. After one year, the lectures were made into a book. That is how it started.

Later on, invitations came from various institutions and organizations, both in America and China. I have spoken at many business schools in China, but what's more interesting is that after the lectures, those entrepreneurs and business people would invite me to talk to them privately. For example, last year in Nanjing, I spoke to about 10 people from cities all over China. We sat around a table and they simply tossed in questions about their real problems, and we discussed what to do.

Liu: Like a consultancy.

Hsu: Like a clinic.

Liu: Do you think a historian is suited to the role of a corporate doctor?

Hsu: I wonder about that too. Nevertheless, I tried my best to look into their problems from theories and cases in history, sociology, and management to analyze their real cases. From time to time I still get emails from some of those who had been in my discussion sessions raising new questions for me to ponder.

To answer your question: I think the huge database accumulated in history includes so many types of organizational issues, the troubles and the possible solutions, which may be adopted as references to analyze organizational problems these businessmen have encountered. I do not answer their questions as a businessman. Rather, I provide them with cases of certain similarities and differences for them to use as references.

Government and Corporation Compared

Liu: You said a country is like a corporation. Could you elaborate?

Hsu: Well, I think you mean a state and a government. They are similar to a corporation and yet they are not quite similar. The similarity is that both governments and corporations are human organizations. However, a government, whether it is a bigger one like China or the United States or a smaller one like Denmark or Switzerland, is a public structure. The power is commissioned by people to have a great enforcing authority. A business is incorporated; it subjugates itself to public law and government interference. A corporation can thus be dissolved and reorganized, but a government cannot be dissolved until the opposition has reached a critical mass to bring about violent change through revolution. An election in a democratic state may change the body and personnel of governance, but not its basic structure. Business corporations are much more susceptible to change—through bankruptcy or a total reorganization, for example.

Liu: Let's talk about it from a leadership perspective. What's the similarity between running a country and running a company?

Hsu: Running a company, no matter how large the company is, has much fewer complications than running a government. But there are similarities. You do need a chief who exercises final authority. You do need a number of assistants as department heads, that is, the division of labor. Among the divisions you do need a chief executive, to run all the daily jobs. So in comparison, the chairman of the board is most like the head of state, and the CEO the government head—those are the two most similar things.

Meanwhile, there are two other things that are similar. Both need somebody to handle the budget and both need to recruit and handle personnel. So the chief executive, the fiscal power, and the personnel power, these three sectors are similar in both types of organization.

The Corporation as Tribe

Liu: You once said that a corporation is also a tribe.

Hsu: Yes, because I see that any corporation is smaller and less-complicated than a state, and a tribe is normally at a sub-state level. A tribe is also more intimate, where people know each other.

The corporation in my mind is family-centered, particularly in Hong Kong, Taiwan, and Southeast Asia. In the United States, you do have the Ford and the Rockefeller families. The Rockefeller family has already separated from business. The Ford family is still in the business. Among the three automobile giants, Ford is the only one that survived. Why? The Ford family injected its own resources into the company to slow the momentum of the collapse. Chrysler and General Motors don't have that. So Ford still represents the family business.

A tribe is more like a family. A corporation is more like a tribe than like a state. In a family-owned corporation, there are certain things you cannot change.

Liu: If we look at a corporation as a tribe, what's the implication here for the business leader?

Hsu: Well, using the case I just mentioned, Ford could survive the crisis because the Ford family has a direct vested interest in the company. In other words, even though Ford's shareholders are scattered all over the place, there is still a hard core that is the Ford family.

In Japan, Mitsubishi or Mitsui or whatever, they have a core. The core is the vested-interest part. The Japanese have an interesting way of choosing leaders in family businesses. They don't need the son to succeed the father. They could have their best partner or employee, who is the best potential CEO, to marry their daughter. That you don't love my daughter doesn't matter. You may have the freedom to have your mistress; meanwhile my daughter has the freedom to have her lover, too. The key is that this kind of family tie makes you adopted as a family member, and an excellent leader chosen by matrimonial ties may represent the core interest of the family business. Good or bad? I don't know. What counts is the stability. But I don't think it is good because money shouldn't always be in the same family.

Liu: I think you've said that in a tribe people are treated as people and you thought that this is a lesson for business leaders.

Hsu: That is how people should be treated, but it is not always what happens.

Liu: In some corporations, people are treated as costs, resources, or capital, but not as people.

Hsu: That's right. They are not instruments. They are people.

I live in Pittsburgh, which was the home base of US Steel until 20 years ago, when the company collapsed. There were so many towns that grew up around a US Steel factory. The factories and communities blended together. The factories took over many functions. They built the school, created the credit union, and operated the food cooperative. They operated like a tribe.

Liu: This is like the state-owned enterprise in China 20 or 30 years ago. So I think we cannot say everything now is better than the past.

Hsu: In Japan not so long ago, a corporation, or *gaisha*, would never lay people off. In times of trouble, the leader could tell workers, "Now we are in a bad year. We all cut our salaries. We cut more, and you cut less because you are a worker and earn less. Let's pass the crisis together. When the crisis is over, we will give back your bonus." For a long time, there were no strikes, because the *gaisha* was a permanent home. It sent wedding gifts and funeral gifts. It took care of orphans and widows. It was a family-centered tribal system.

It was good and bad. Bad because it was almost feudalistic—you depend on it so much; you are tied to it. Good because you really got taken care of. There is always a good part and a bad part.

Leadership in the New Heterarchy

Liu: People are saying that the world is fundamentally different from 500 years ago, or 50 years ago. If a great leader from 500 years ago were landed here, what would he do differently?

Hsu: Through different kinds of institutionalized or cultural education, even in the underdeveloped countries of today's world, people have a kind of conscience that human beings should be treated as human beings and not stratified into different castes or classes. This makes everybody want to be his or her own master. This awareness makes people today more inclined to have a free and fluid—rather than an organized, stabilized, or crystallized—organization. This inclination will change what has been taken for granted about organizations, and what they were supposed to be throughout thousand years of human history.

In the past the organizational structure was a hierarchy with several levels, like a pyramid. You put a stone somewhere and it sticks there. For centuries and millennia in the past, almost all types of organized institutions, corporations, schools, armies, bureaucracies, have had a pyramid structure. We want to change that. Instead of a hierarchy, we may adopt a structure called a heterarchy. Where a hierarchy is a structure in which power is divided along strata, a heterarchy has power being shared among sectors of some varieties. A pile of the hierarchy becomes strings or clusters in the heterarchy.

We see this coming with the outsourcing phenomenon. In America, if you make a phone call to customer service, the chances are that the call is answered in India or the Philippines. I believe my income tax is calculated in India. Heterarchy is going to be the pattern.

Heterarchy can be observed in anthropology and archeology, in particular, as an alternative to hierarchy in human history. We can observe how clusters and interdependent communities supplement each other, in a symbiotic relationship.

Liu: So leadership is moving from the old command-and-control style to something more collaborative?

Hsu: Collaboration must involve negotiation. Ideally, at every link of the cluster, there should be two or more upstream links to choose from, and two or more downstream links to choose from. At each link, people ought to have the freedom to choose, and be subjected to other people's choices too. You must compete with other people to please your downstream partners.

Superficially, breaking things down into fragments may appear to leave them vulnerable. Looked at more positively, you give everybody some freedom to develop and have options. The size of each segment is much smaller—ideally, a constitution of two or three levels: a commander, two supervisors, and floor workers who can be upgraded to supervisors too. You don't have the bureaucratic behavior, and you don't have the wasted energy and time of passing information along numerous layers. The leader becomes the one who negotiates on your behalf, and the profit or interest is shared immediately. You don't need to wait, making everybody more independent.

Liu: And we need more leaders because we have more segments of smaller size.

Hsu: Yes, many, many leaders. I call this *qunlong wushou*, which is from *the Book of Changes*, meaning "many dragons without the leading one." We always speak of *feilong zaitian*, "a gigantic, powerful dragon flying augustly in the sky," which looks very good but actually is no good. It leads to *kanglong youhui*, "the arrogant, high-flying dragon being shamed by its failure." The heterarchical structure is a phenomenon of *qunlong wushou* so that every single dragon flies his or her own way. By having a free selection of collaborators, with more options, the individual participant may enjoy more options and freedoms than a worker in a gigantic bureaucracy of today's business world.

Liu: Therefore a heterarchy would provide more flexibility?

Hsu: Yes. With the changes in modern science and technology being very rapid, such a heterarchy may easily adopt new technology by making changes only in certain sections rather than restructuring the entire huge system, as modern industries are compelled to do.

Look at the experience of the collapse of the steel industry in Pittsburgh. These steel mills were so integrated and so huge that if a certain segment had to be upgraded, it would be hard to change only that given segment as the entire process had been tied together into one system. It ended up that these mills had to put off necessary improvements to the point where they had to be given up completely and new mills would be built somewhere else. In the heterarchy model, each module stands alone, while numerous relatively independent modules are linked to constitute a chain of production.

Therefore, any of these modules may be upgraded in order to take advantage of technological progress; and rather than having to tear down the rest of the chain, only minor adjustments are necessary along the way. In times of rapid technological advancement, such flexibility should be appreciated.

13

Debashis Chatterjee: Leading Consciously

Debashis Chatterjee is currently the Director of the Indian Institute of Management (IIM), Kozhikode, having taught for more than a decade in IIM in Lucknow and Calcutta. He was recently a Visiting Fulbright Professor at Harvard University's Kennedy School of Government, and has taught in the MBA programs at the University of St. Thomas in Minnesota and at Harvard Business School. His books include *Leading Consciously* (1998), *Light the Fire in Your Heart* (2004), *Break Free* (2006) and *Timeless Leadership: 18 Leadership Sutras from the Bhagavad Gita* (forthcoming).

Where China is often compared to the "dragon," India is the "elephant" and there is currently a great deal of debate over which will dominate the economic world in the future. While it has been many decades since Westerners first began to learn the management and leadership wisdom encapsulated in the strategies of Sun Tzu and in ancient Chinese traditions, it is only comparatively recently that they began to look to the spiritual wisdom in the ancient Indian traditions and apply it to business and leadership. In 2006, *Business-Week* reported the movement of "Karma Capitalism," since when Indian wisdom, along with its economic development, has attracted increasing attention.

Debashis Chatterjee, a long-time advocate of the need for a new model of leadership, is well positioned to ride this wave of enthusiasm for timeless leadership wisdom. He spoke to me about his ideas on leadership over the phone from Kozhikode, India, in December 2009.

Leadership Wisdom in the Indian Tradition

Liu: When did you start becoming interested in management and leadership?

Chatterjee: I started when I took my first corporate job for an organization of 100,000 people. My lessons in management first came from serving in this big Indian company, which was almost like a microcosm of what happens when different kinds of people have to work together towards a common purpose.

Then I thought an MBA degree might help me make better sense of organizations. But when I went for an MBA in the Indian Institute of Management, I realized that they were teaching pretty much what Harvard and MIT would be teaching. There was hardly anything "Indian" about the Indian Institute of Management.

So I decided to try my luck at MIT and Harvard. Luckily I got a Fulbright Fellowship twice, one pre-doctoral and the other post-doctoral, which landed me both in MIT and Harvard.

Liu: And there you met Peter Senge.

Chatterjee: Yes. I was lucky to meet Peter Senge. He had published *The Fifth Discipline*, which was absolutely the rage at that time. I did a little review of that book, in which I said, "Systems thinking alone does not solve problems. Systems feeling has to come along with systems thinking because there are a few systems you don't change—unless there is a change of heart." Senge noticed it and he said, "Debashis, if you could write what you have to say in the form of a book, I would be happy to do a foreword." So I wrote the whole book, *Leading Consciously*, in 17 or 18 days and it was published in 1998, primarily because of Senge's patronage.

In that book, I argue for looking at the huge amount of wisdom in the Indian tradition and applying it in management and leadership.

Like in most countries which were colonized before, in India once an idea is endorsed by America or England it gets more accepted. Since I got the endorsement from Harvard and MIT and I was also doing programs for Motorola when I was in the United States, the book began to circulate not just around the world but also in India. People began to understand that Indian wisdom can be explored to find solutions to our corporate problems. I am proud that I could influence my own people in a way that I hadn't thought I could.

Inclusive and Vertical: The Indian Orientation toward Capitalism

Liu: It is ironic that you went to the West and rediscovered the Indian wisdom there instead. I can see that Westerners are paying attention. In 2006, *BusinessWeek* magazine published an article saying that an Indian management model, which it called "Karma Capitalism," was catching on. This model of capitalism pursues purpose as well as profit, and serves stakeholders as well as shareholders. As an Indian management professor who has taught both in India and in the United States, to what extent do you agree with this observation?

Chatterjee: I only partly agree with it. What we call the models of Indian organizations are largely Western. They are British and American in their structures. They have the same division of labor and the same orientation toward management as the Western organizations have. However, the people who work in these organizations are very different from their Western counterparts. These people are not in the transactional model of relationships; they are in more relational mode, like people in most of Asia would be.

The phrase "Karma Capitalism" seems to me simply another very popular Western way of classifying a very complex civilization like India. You can't have one label for China called "Red Book Management." It doesn't say much about China. "Karma Capitalism" says only a little bit about India. The word "karma" is not even properly understood by the Western psyche: it means much more than just fate or whatever import that the Western world has given it.

When you talk about purpose, the Indian orientation is essentially the evolution of the person—that is the ultimate purpose. Why should I work for an organization? Because it helps me evolve as a person. This is a very different orientation. When I say I am a person, my boundary between the person and the community is not as strong as it would be in the Western sense. So for me the person and the community are pretty much inclusive concepts. For instance, our surnames are actually based on *gotras*. In Vedic Sanskrit, the word *gotra* originally meant "cow-pen." Cows were at the time the most valuable possession of a family group, so with time, the term *gotra* began to refer to the family group who owned a particular pen of cows. The term was associated eventually with just the family group and its lineage. *Gotras* are also named after ancient Indian sages or *rishis*. In Maharashtra, Western India, you will find people who have got their surnames from the names of the villages they come from.

So the orientation toward community has been part of the Indian psyche. When we talk of "karma," we talk about the collective, the larger aspect, not just the individual's personal trajectory in life. When we talk about the individual, we talk about the individual as indivisible from the community.

Liu: So you don't agree with the label "Karma Capitalism," but you do agree that in India people have a completely different orientation toward business from the people in the West.

Chatterjee: Yes, quite significantly so.

Liu: Actually C. K. Prahalad, an influential management thinker of Indian descent who teaches in the West, also said that it would be better called "inclusive capitalism." What do you think of this name?

Chatterjee: I agree to some extent because the word "inclusive" means that you include the community. I would add one more dimension and say inclusive and "vertical." By "vertical" we are talking about the evolution from being just sensory human beings with a psycho-physical structure to a higher spiritual dimension—which is our shared human heritage.

For instance, the role models of leadership in India have been people like Mahatma Gandhi, J. R. D. Tata of the Tata Group and Narayana Murthy of Infosys. These people have had sacrifice and renunciation as a common streak in their character. They follow the same paradigm, which means that the leader is the trustee of wealth and he is a trustee because he stands in trust with the rest of the community. He holds in trust the wealth which is not his personal property. What does he get out of holding wealth in trust? Well, he evolves as a person vertically, and the community trusts him more for it. So sacrifice does not necessarily mean giving up; it means taking something higher and that the lower appetites for personal possession and all of that fall off by themselves.

"Renunciation" is a very important word for India. It means not sacrificing alone but evolving to a higher plane of living and perception. Therefore a typical Indian leader will be half sage and half king. He's got a kingdom but it will not be his personal wealth, but the community wealth that he holds in trust. All our major role models in India have more or less followed that dimension. So I would add one more aspect to what Prahalad said and call it an inclusive and vertical orientation toward capitalism.

The Inner Side of Leadership

Liu: You have already touched on my next question. I would like to talk about leadership more specifically. How is leadership viewed differently in India than in the United States?

Chatterjee: From a critical perspective, it's the social orientation of a leader that's very important in the United States. For instance, the American presidential election is largely a contest of packaging. The quality of the packaging is important because a leader is supposed to be socially savvy. It's very important for them to be savvy to be able to win an election.

In India a leader is viewed not just as a social entity. He is viewed from his internal orientation and his commitment to the truth. If you look at our prime minister, he is respected primarily because of his personal conduct. He is a very qualified economist, with degrees from Cambridge and Oxford, yet India adores him for his simplicity. He is not very socially savvy, not a great orator or anything. But he is somebody whose integrity is deep and beyond question.

So India has always looked at the inner side of leadership a lot more. Our role models are not very impressive to look at from the social context, but some of them are extremely impressive in terms of their personal integrity, their commitment to the sync between beliefs and actions, the inner work of purification of personal greed, and all of that.

Liu: So you are saying that in leadership, Indian people pay more attention to character and values?

Chatterjee: A lot more than one would superficially think. The kind of value they pay attention to is not necessarily material value. They would pay attention to some of those higher-order values that are more intangible and therefore more potent and powerful.

For example, democracy has functioned for such a long time in India. The value of democracy is very deeply entrenched in the Indian psyche. I think democracy in India is understood very differently from the understanding in the Western context. India has got a different orientation toward democracy and leaders have to understand it. Democracy means that we are all of the one same spirit. So at the human level we are all one, but not necessarily at the social and economic levels. That's where the Indian definition of democracy is unique and leaders have to understand and pay due attention to that.

Leadership is a State of Consciousness

Liu: In the prelude to *Leading Consciously*, after quoting Rabindranath Tagore, who said that each one of us is the supreme leader in his or her own kingdom, you said that "Leadership is not a science or an art, it is a state of consciousness in which we discover the path to our own kingdoms." Could you elaborate on this? How do you define leadership?

Chatterjee: I define it in one simple sentence. I think that the task of the leader is to lead people to themselves.

Liu: Lead people to be themselves?

Chatterjee: Lead people to their own selves—to their own magnificence as spiritual beings in the human form. This is the number-one job of a leader. Number two is that leaders attend to human sufferings. We do not always suffer from economic deprivation; we suffer because of tags, titles, and so on; we suffer because we can't grow to our own potential for some reason. So we all have different kinds of sufferings.

I think the real job of a leader is to address human suffering in terms of people not being able to reach their full potential. If the leader did not address the human suffering he would not be a leader for long because, eventually, it is in the human context that I look at the leadership largely. I don't look at leadership from the point of view of business performance, because performance comes when human beings within the organization reach their full potential. So, it is the leader's job to enable people to arrive at their ultimate potential, to remove their sufferings and those blocks for them to actualize their full potential.

Liu: How do you connect this with the statement "leadership is a state of consciousness?"

Chatterjee: Only when people are conscious of the fact that all human beings have capabilities are they able to be themselves. See, we all have our own capabilities and talents, but if we demand from a person what is not his natural quality, if we ask a horse to fly or a bird to run, we will do disservice both to the horse and the bird. Most modern organizations don't seem to understand that organizations are created for people and not people for organizations. This is India's greatest difference from the Western paradigm.

In the West, they say "I think therefore I am;" in India we say "I am therefore I think." So my being, my being alive, and my being human, is a primary condition for me to be a member of an organization. If I am a member of an organization, it is the organization's job to create for me a job profile which is natural and spontaneously aligned with my talents and my gifts. So if I don't change the organization to suit the individuals' natural capabilities, then I am doing disservice to the individuals. That's where consciousness is very critical: am I conscious of the person I am dealing with in the context of the organization? Business grows because people grow the business. We often say "the customer comes first." Indians would tend to believe that the human being comes first—the customer is merely a nomenclature.

Conscious Leaders in the World

Liu: Could you give me an example of this "Conscious Leadership?"

Chatterjee: J. R. D. Tata was an example. He was the architect of the Tata empire; literally he brought the Tata name worldwide. There is a little story about him when he was visiting a plant furnace in Jamshedpur in Eastern India. He was about to be shown around the furnace by an engineer who had got all the specifications about the furnace, the temperature, the construction, and all the technical features. The engineer was waiting for Tata to ask questions about all these, but he was surprised that Tata had only one question to ask. The question was: "How will that human being who will operate that plant furnace be able to stand in front of the tremendous heat the furnace will have? Have you thought of that human being? How will he actually operate the furnace?" This was the only question.

On another occasion, some employees were on strike and demonstrating with slogans and flags outside. He looked at them and talked personally to the HR manager: "Look," he said, "they have the right to demonstrate, but they should not demonstrate like that under the hot sun. Why don't you give them a cold drink and ask them to stand in the shade? I am not taking over their right to protest, but making them a little more comfortable so that they are treated as human beings, not just as protesting laborers."

This is the Indian orientation: a state of consciousness. We are talking about being conscious of a human being behind the action, not just a designation or a role. That's very important for the Indian context.

Liu: Are there other examples of conscious leaders among current business leaders, either in the East or in the West?

Chatterjee: John Mackey of Whole Foods is one, Ray Anderson of Interface is another, and Narayana Murthy of Infosys, Ho Kwon Ping of Banyan Tree in Singapore . . . You tell me how many names you want!

Liu: So "Conscious Leadership" is not something only made in India?

Chatterjee: India has a well-articulated wisdom basis for it, but it can be anywhere in the world. Consciousness is not an Indian property, but its thought system grew in India. Just as America is very motor-concentrated, but cars can be crafted anywhere, so this body of knowledge grew up in India, but can be applied anywhere else.

Liu: Do we see more conscious leaders in India than in other countries?

Chatterjee: There is this likelihood because that is part of our self, but not necessarily so. It can happen anywhere else in the world because wisdom cannot come with geography. You can't say American wisdom or Chinese wisdom. Wisdom is wisdom. America applies it. China applies it. It is the same wisdom.

Applying Consciousness in Business

Liu: You mentioned that you didn't particularly talk about leadership in a business context. Do you find it difficult when you talk to business executives around the world for them to understand this idea of "Conscious Leadership?"

Chatterjee: Yes and no. They do find it difficult to relate it to their immediate work, but at the personal level, most of them are completely convinced that this is true. You are talking to them on the basis of truth, not convenience. But they don't know how that truth will apply to their work, and that's where the challenge is.

Liu: And how do you help them face that challenge?

Chatterjee: Essentially I say to them, "If you are convinced that this is the truth, then why don't you organize around some of this truth, if not in your current organization, at least in your personal life? So this is essentially testing the truth in a safe environment first. And then bring it out to the field of business, which is where you are."

Our environment is who we are. When we change, our environment also changes. So, it looks very difficult on the face of it, but it might not be that difficult when we have transformed ourselves. Let me give you a metaphor. There is a room that is dark and you are thinking about how to deal with the darkness. All of a sudden you realize that all you need is a flash of light, because the darkness is never there, it is only a perception. Darkness is the absence of light. At the moment I have the illumination of that light, immediately what seems dark is no longer dark.

So, what prevents them from actually believing in it in the working organization is the lack of the right knowledge in the right context. When they experiment with this idea, as many of the managers and my students do, then they realize it works, not just in personal life, but also in organizational life. You need to try it out.

Because the way organizations are constructed is not based on this truth, we have to reconstruct these organizations. Organizations will be very different in the next 100 years. There is a movement now in corporate America called "Conscious Capitalism." John Mackey of Whole Foods, Ray Anderson of Interface, and several others are involved in it. Some people are now changing the way organizations will be. The history of organizations is not finished yet. You and I are in the process of creating a new story for them.

The Caste System and Conscious Leadership

Liu: You are saying that "Conscious Leadership" is about the realization of human potential.

Chatterjee: That's true.

Liu: In India, there is something that makes me uncomfortable and also seems to be in serious conflict with the idea of "Conscious Leadership": the caste system which divides people into different categories. If you are born into one category, you are noble forever. If you are born into another, you are humble forever. Could you comment on that?

Chatterjee: The caste structure is a social construct. There are people who are traditionally good at something. Say, the laborers would go out and work with their hands, so they are good at those manual skills, and they would belong to that caste. There are people who are good at thinking, and they would become the high caste of the Brahmin. This social structure came from an individual's orientation, you know, different talents and capabilities. Unfortunately the caste system that was created later on in India has actually perverted that division of talents and capabilities into a structure based on exploitation and vested interest. But that's not what the caste structure means.

The caste structure means that human potential is multiple and varied and expresses itself in multiple ways. Someone can be good at cognitive processing, someone can be good at manual dexterity, and someone can be good at trade and service. So the four castes are actually four different human capabilities, but it has become an ossified social structure, with all its negativities.

Originally the caste was about your own potential and the way to maximize your own potential. But the original intent got destroyed and perverted by people who wanted to hold onto the system although they did not have the potential. If you do not have the potential to be a Brahmin, which is the highest caste, you still want to be a Brahmin because of the privileges that go with it. The original intent was very clear. It was about the four different ways that human beings expressed their potential in a collective system.

Liu: You were saying that the caste structure was originally good, but not good now?

Chatterjee: It is good only when you understand it consciously, bad when you start replicating that unconsciously. The caste is almost gone in India: a large percentage of Indians don't subscribe to that caste system.

Liu: If a person is born into the lowest caste, is it possible for him or her to make it to be a professor in India?

Chatterjee: In modern India, yes, most certainly so. In India 100 years back, unlikely. Right now I am the CEO of one of India's most prestigious national business schools—the IIM—and we have an affirmative-action policy. We have compulsory reservation for people of certain castes. We are doing our best to be inclusive—to set right the social system.

Leaders Work on the System and Create History

Liu: Do you differentiate between leadership and management?

Chatterjee: I do. Managers work within the system; leaders work on the system—that's the primary difference. Leaders can see a large system, because they have what is called "systems sensitivity," much more than the managers have. A manager is actually caught up in the operational and procedural details so much that his systems sensitivity is not always clearly honed, more so in the human context. A manager does not always necessarily have an insight as to how a large number of people will behave as a system. Leaders are really good at comprehending people's systems and working on them.

Liu: You once told a story about Gandhi. When a history professor challenged the concept of non-violence based on his "knowledge of history," Gandhi answered, "Sir, your job is to teach history while mine is to create it." I think this is in the same sense of the leadership/management difference; is that right?

Chatterjee: That's right—it can be right not just for Gandhi but also for anyone with a similar state of consciousness. You create history not just by yourself, but by energizing the people around you to perform much better than they would without you. You become conscious of their potential, and you activate that potential so the history is created by them. You don't singlehandedly create history. You create history through your people. That's exactly what Gandhi and many others did.

Indians Look for Spiritual Strength in Their Leaders

Liu: As you probably know, worldwide research by Jim Kouzes and Barry Posner found that the top four qualities that people expect from good leaders is that they are honest, forward-looking, inspiring, and competent. In *Leading Consciously*, you quote survey results showing that 1,000 managers in 12 Indian organizations selected the following as the top five attributes of a good leader: dynamism, inspiring character, vision, ethical values, and spiritual strength. What strikes me at the first glance is that most items in the two sets of results are the same.

Chatterjee: Yes, they are timeless.

Liu: But there are still differences. The major difference is in the Indian people's emphasis on spiritual strength and the lack of attention to competence. Would you like to comment on that?

Chatterjee: In the classical Indian thinking, competence comes from knowledge. Competence comes from not just the mind which gives knowledge, but also that which stands behind knowledge, which is wisdom. If I am very competent in shooting skills, I may get the Olympic gold medal, but I can also kill people if I don't have the wisdom. So competence not backed by wisdom is incompetence; efficiency not backed by wisdom is inefficiency. If the same competence is applied in a negative sense; it will be even more dangerous for the world.

Look at 9/11. Those behind 9/11 were very competent and educated people. Most of the world's problems today are created by very competent people. When you have competence without wisdom it is very, very difficult to remain competent.

So I look at wisdom as the primary driver. When India says that spiritual illumination is very important, we are essentially talking about competence which is evolutionary, which makes the world grow as we grow, rather than that we destroy the world and grow at the expense of the universe and planetary system. That's not competence at all; that's inefficiency.

Much of what goes out as efficiency is not efficiency at all, including the GDP figures that we have. That's not a measure of efficiency, but a measure of immense depletion of the world's natural resources. In India, it raises the question: "Are we getting the competence on sustainable bases or is the competence becoming incompetence in the long run?" That's the question we have to ask about the way businesses have moved in the last 1,500 years.

Liu: Instead of competence, Indian people look for spiritual strength in leaders. Why is that?

Chatterjee: India is traditionally oriented toward spirituality, because this country would not survive without that spiritual strength. Look at the 800 million people, living for $2 or less a day. That is the kind of material deprivation you see in India. What keeps them alive is hope: the physical body and the mind are only temporary phenomena; and it is going to change for the better if they do good, if they work harder, if they are honest, if they actually serve their God.

So there is an evolutionary urge in all of them, although their material conditions are very poor. What keeps them alive is the spiritual strength. This is the basis of Indian resilience and democracy. You see, whether we fight with each other, whether we kill each other, whatever happens, we have also to honor the fact that we are spiritual beings first and material beings later. So that identification with spiritual strength has given us the resilience that we have as a country and as a culture. That is our greatest strength.

But it can also be our weakness if we do not develop the spiritual values into material wealth for the large number of people. When we hold wealth and do not share, that's not spiritual. There are still companies where, before they start work in the morning, people worship their machines like they worship a god or a goddess. Everywhere you go in India, you'll see the impact of spiritual values which are very deeply embedded in the Indian psyche.

Liu: People are beginning to talk now about spiritual intelligence. Do you believe that aside from intellectual intelligence and emotional intelligence, there is spiritual intelligence? And is it important to leadership?

Chatterjee: Yes, it is important because spiritual intelligence is a collective intelligence of the whole, of the entire cosmic and planetary system. Spiritual intelligence says that whatever is good for the large is good for the small. It has a very inclusive way of looking at reality. It says that if it is good for the world it must be good for the country, not the other way around. You know, ultimately this will turn out to be true.

Liu: In the United States and the West in general, people are religious as well. On this basis, can we say that both Indian and Western people are strong at this spiritual intelligence?

Chatterjee: Religion is different from spirituality. Religion is an organization; spirituality is a state of consciousness. You can't mix the two. Religion is a structure of words, habits, rituals, and a way of accessing spirituality. It is like a ladder and spirituality is like the plane that you access via the ladder.

In the United States, very often religion is for Sundays, when one goes to church. It is divorced from work and life. In India, religion is integrated with work and life, and that's what makes India spiritual in the true sense. Spirituality means that at every moment of my living I will live that religion. Religion lives not just in the church, not just in the temple, not just in the mosque. Only when it lives in my everyday activity, when it lives within me as a state of the consciousness of the whole, can I say I am spiritual. So in the United States and Western Europe, spirituality is not quite there in everyday life. There is only a codified form, which is what religion is. Spirituality is free from codes and dogmas. Religion is codified and breeds dogmas.

We are all spiritual but we might not be religious. For instance, I am not religious, but I am spiritual. I don't go to the temple every day, but I attend to my consciousness on an every-moment basis.

Leadership Lessons from the *Bhagavad Gita*

Liu: I know you are writing a leadership book based on the *Bhagavad Gita*, a book with a history of thousands of years. Could you give me a little preview: What are the major leadership lessons from the *Bhagavad Gita* for our current context?

Chatterjee: The number one lesson is that we have to align our personal selfish will with the will of the larger planet and the larger cosmos. The *Gita* is talking about two characters, Arjuna and Krishna, who are at two different stages of consciousness.

Arjuna is lost in the middle of a battle. He thinks that he cannot kill somebody else as he sees these adversaries as different from himself and therefore he is paralyzed in action. His consciousness is limited to his mind, which divides. Krishna is his charioteer and counselor, a divine being in disguise. Krishna is telling him, "Look, those people that you see as adversaries are neither adversaries nor friends. They are you, yourself. Killing, war, destruction, and devastation also happen in nature. But when they happen for the larger purpose, then this is the right thing to happen at that point in time." Say, when an earthquake happens, you can't say, "Why did this earthquake happen?" You know it is a happening. It's a reality.

So the *Gita* is a book about being real. It says, "Anything that prevents me from being real is my acquired nature." Arjuna represents the acquired nature: he has become a fighter; he has some ideas; he has some educated guesses about reality. But Krishna is saying, "Be spontaneous. Be absolutely natural. Be your own self. When you are your own self, you'll see that fighting the battle is not going to be that difficult because through this battle you are going to evolve as a person, and you are going to evolve into your natural self."

That's the message of the *Gita*. The fight is happening in the mind, where there are a million mutinies and those mutinies have to be sorted out before we become an integrated being. That would align us with the whole of the cosmos, and when we become that, all the conflicts within us would have been resolved. The real war in the *Gita* is a war in the human mind. That's where the solution to the world's problems has to be found. The *Gita* is a hugely contemporary text although it was written thousands of years ago. It is as contemporary as you can imagine.

The Indian Leadership Style

Liu: I know very little about India, although we are neighbors. To my knowledge, there are many sub-cultures in India.

Chatterjee: That's true: 1.2 billion people, 75 major political parties, and 500 different ways of cooking rice!

Liu: So, is there an Indian style of leadership, or are there many leadership styles?

Chatterjee: There are several leadership styles but all of them converge on a few things. One, the human being comes before the system. What we have is a human-centered civilization. Two, the collective is more important than the individual. Three, emotions are very critical in dealing with people. We deal with several layers of emotions on a daily basis—some explicit, some subtle and unexpressed.

Liu: In Japan, too, the collective comes before the individual. Is there any difference?

Chatterjee: It has similarities with the Japanese style, but we are far more tolerant in forging this collectivity. We have a lot more complexities than Japan has because of the number of cultures and sub-cultures. Forging collectivity takes a lot more time in India. India is a slow-moving elephant, like our GDP, but it moves, and then collectivity is forged and the movement becomes more spontaneous. You see Europe has gotten fragmented in less than 100 years. The united Europe does not stand any more, but the united India has survived for God-knows-how-many thousands of years now. In India, it is a slow but deeply integrating process.

Liu: And from your understanding, what's the difference between the Indian and Chinese leadership styles?

Chatterjee: I think that it is an ideology that unites China more than the spiritual dimension. That unity is forged more at the mental level rather than at the spiritual level. The Chinese are far more capable of acting together than Indians are. This is the advantage of China. In China, action precedes thought. In India, a lot of thought has to go in before action starts.

India is more thought-driven and China is more action-oriented. You see our businesses: their global imprint is largely through leadership in the intellectual-property sector and all of that. For China, manufacturing is the leading thing.

Liu: We admire India for that part actually.

Chatterjee: We admire China for what we are missing too. We realize that manufacturing is our missed bus, and we don't want to miss it.

Let me tell you, the reason for India's growth spurt is China. We asked, "If China can do it, why can't we?" China spurs us on. We never said "If America can do it, why can't we?" We chose China because China is so close to us. However, our growth trajectory will be different from China; we will grow more slowly and perhaps more steadily than China has.

Looking into the future, people often say either India or China will dominate. That doesn't surprise me at all. What surprises me is why they were asleep for so long. We have actually poked each other into some kind of reselection. We have been complementary, nudging each other to evolve. I think that's the great part.

Liu: You mentioned earlier that Peter Senge wrote a foreword for one of your books. He actually wrote one of mine too. In his foreword to my *Master Classes of Leadership*, published recently in China, he wrote, "My personal belief is that it will be this traditional knowledge of China and India, largely lost today in the mad dash toward modernization, that will prove far more important than their economic muscle and burgeoning markets. We need a new tradition of leadership that is meaningful across all cultures and that interconnects the multiple domains of our existence in ways that consumerism and industrial growth never have."

Chatterjee: Exactly, right there.

Liu: That makes our conversation very important.

Chatterjee: Absolutely so.

Endnote

1 Pete Engardio with Jena McGregor, "Karma Capitalism," *BusinessWeek*, October 30, 2006.

Beyond the American Model

A recurring theme of these conversations, perhaps unduly overshadowed by others, is that leadership can be culture-specific. Since the fundamental issues of leadership are simply echoes of the critical issues of life, we won't expect them to be treated the same way across the globe. In assembling this book, I have tried to bring leadership thinkers from Europe, China, and India together with those from the United States. Although the conversations literally took place between each Master and me, an attentive reader might be able to hear the Masters having virtual dialogs across different cultures. Such cross-cultural exchanges on leadership, especially those between the East and the West, have been regrettably rare, partly because leadership, as both a research subject and training business, has been to a large extent an American product.

A bias in this field, which is often an American one, is to claim the universality of findings based on a small sample within a specific context. To take but one example, the renowned Warren Bennis, one of the Masters in this book, after studying two groups of leaders—the young *geeks* and the old *geezers*, but both American—discovered that all those leaders share four basic qualities. He and his co-author then asserted: "We are now convinced that these four qualities mark all exemplary leaders, whatever their age, era, gender, ethnicity, or race."[1]

This kind of confidence might only reflect a rhetorical art, but it might also reveal a profound belief, and probably a well-grounded one. As in other human activities, there is timeless and borderless wisdom in leadership. A sage in ancient China said, "There are sages in the East. There are sages in the West. The mind is the same. The reasoning is the same. If these are not the same, they are not sages." Therefore it is justifiable to have this universality bias, from which I couldn't exempt myself when I endeavored to present the Eight Disciplines of Leadership.

As with many other human activities, however, leadership is culture-specific. The leader, the community the leader is leading, the purpose for which the leader is leading, and the context in which the leader is leading, are all intertwined, and all can have cultural implications that are significant to activities of leadership. Even if the four qualities that Warren Bennis found or the eight disciplines that I summarized are universal—and I believe they are to a certain extent—people in different cultures certainly prioritize them in different hierarchies, interpret them with different meanings, and implement them in different ways. Thus cultural sensitivity, or cultural intelligence, is essential in leadership. One of my favorite books is *Riding the Waves of Culture* by Fons Trompenaars and Charles Hampden-Turner, in which the two European authors, following the tradition of the cross-cultural management guru Geert Hofstede (another European), eloquently argue that there is no one best way of management, or leadership.

If we embrace the view that leadership is culture-specific, then we face three challenges, for which there are no easy solutions.

The first of these challenges is to find *your own* best way, the one that suits your cultural context. Peter Drucker, my favorite management writer, clearly didn't subscribe to the one-best-way-of-leadership school of thought when he wrote the following words in the 1980s:

> Because management deals with the integration of people in a common venture, it is deeply embedded in culture. What managers do in West Germany, in Britain, in the United States, in Japan, or in Brazil is exactly the same. How they do it may be quite different. Thus one of the basic challenges

managers in a developing country face is to find and identify those parts of their own tradition, history, and culture that can be used as management building blocks.[2]

The second challenge is to lead in a cross-cultural context, an undertaking more demanding than ever due to the integration of the global economy, the advancement of communications and transportation, and other factors that contribute to the popular phrase "the world is flat." This task falls in the domain of cross-cultural management, where scholars like Hofstede and Trompenaars have provided a great number of insights.

The third challenge I would like to stress here is to make a cultural "paradigm shift" in leadership. This will entail that we absorb leadership wisdom from other cultures and integrate it into our own. In particular, it means that the American model of leadership, which has dominated the world both as a school of thought and a guide for practice for the past several decades, should upgrade itself by learning from other cultures.

The fact that the recent financial meltdown originated in the United States is just one striking piece of evidence for the malfunctioning of the American leadership model. Many observers in the United States have sensed it too. For example, the Harvard Business School dean Jay Light wrote in November 2008: "Who bears responsibility for the collapse of 2008? It is a collective failure, not only of financial safeguards and institutions, but of leadership at many levels. This was true in corporate executive offices, in government, and yes—in business schools too."[3] Yet Jay Light still had the view of an insider, which perhaps prevented him from taking the next logical step and saying "It is a failure of leadership—of the American model."

To recapitulate the gist of such a model exceeds both the capacity of this Afterword and the capability of its author. Instead I will just make two points.

My first point is that in such a model, people usually justify great actions in terms of great consequences. They do things because they expect good results. Based on his observations of such a model, James March, another of the Masters in this book, suggests that leaders learn from Don Quixote, who replaces the logic of consequence with the logic of identity, or who acts according to "who I am" rather than "what I can get." In cultural terms, such a model is more achievement-oriented than the ascription-oriented model common in Eastern cultures.

My second point is that in such a model, people tend to confront nature and try to take advantage of it, rather than to live harmoniously with it, or to see humanity and nature as an integrated whole as many Eastern cultures do. Peter Senge, another of the Masters in this book and one of the few influential Western management gurus with a deep understanding of Eastern wisdom traditions, quotes Zhang Zai, a Confucian scholar who lived nearly a millennium ago:

> Heaven is my father and Earth is my mother, and even such a small creature as I finds an intimate place in their midst. Therefore that which fills the universe I regard as my body and that which directs the universe I consider my nature. All people are my brothers and sisters, and all things are my companions.

Reading this, Senge says,

> . . . it brings to mind the wisdom tradition of native people around the world, who have been chiding modern Western civilization for centuries that it must set itself right in terms of seeing ourselves as part of, not apart from, the larger living world. While these native traditions are also important, they are unlikely to kindle a widespread awakening because they have, sadly, been marginalized by industrial expansion and the subjugation of native peoples. But China and India are already shaping the twenty-first century and are likely to play an even larger role in the coming decades. What would happen if they simultaneously did so while awakening to their own wisdom traditions and blending these with wisdom from the West? This would truly be leadership for the world, not just in the world.[4]

While Peter Senge was rightly pushing Easterners to awaken to their wisdom traditions and blend these with those of the West, I would like to propose here that Westerners awaken to Eastern wisdom traditions and blend these with their own. It is a challenge beyond the scope of this book. Nevertheless I hope it can be a starting point. In the beginning of this book, I invited you to join in those conversations and act on those leadership disciplines. Now, I extend another invitation to a new intellectual and developmental journey, an exploration of culturally integrated "leadership for the world." Join me.

Beijing, May 2010

Endnotes

1 Warren Bennis and Robert Thomas, *Leading for a Lifetime* (Harvard Business School Press, 2007), ix.
2 Peter Drucker, *The New Realities* (Transaction Publishers, 2003), 221.
3 Jay Light, "The Leadership Imperative," http://www.forbes.com/2008/11/19/harvard-leadership-education-oped-cx_teachable08_jol_1119light.html.
4 Peter Senge, "Leadership for the World," foreword to Lan Liu's *Master Classes of Leadership* (Beijing: China Citic Press, 2009).

Index